BASQUE ECONOMY

Mikel Gómez Uranga is a professor in the Department of Applied Economics at the University of the Basque Country, where he has been teaching for twenty years. His research interests include economics and technical change and regional studies. He is also involved in the development of institutional and evolutionary economics and has been visiting professor at the University of Lyon and the University of Nevada.

He has recently served as coordinator and researcher for the Basque Country in several research projects financed by the European Commission, such as the "VALUE Program," "Regional Innovation Systems: Designing for the Future," and "Universities, Technology Transfer, and Spin-off Activities" (1996–98).

His major recent publications are "Regional Systems of Innovation: An Evolutionary Perspective," *Environment and Planning A* 30:1563–1584, 1998, coauthor; "Non-redistributing Prices and Exclusion in the Evolution of Internet," *Journal of Economic Issues*, December 1998, no. 4; *Soberanía económica y globalización en Euskal Herria*, Manu Robles-Arangiz Institutua, 1998, coeditor and coauthor; book review of R. Mansel and U. Wehn's *Knowledge Societies: Information Technology for Sustainable Development* (1998, Oxford University Press), *Journal of Economic Issues*, September 1999, no. 3; "Panorama of the Basque Country and its Competence for Self-Government," *European Planning Studies* 8(4):521–535, 2000, coauthor.

Mikel Gómez Uranga

Basque Economy
from Industrialization to Globalization

Basque Textbooks Series

Xabier Barrutia, Anton Borja, Goio Etxebarria,
Helena Franco, Begoña Garcia-Saenz, Mikel Gómez
Uranga, Yolanda Jubeto, Garikoitz Otazua, Eva Velasco,
and Mikel Zurbano participated in writing this book.

Translated into English by Ana Olabe.

Center for Basque Studies
University of Nevada, Reno

This book was published with generous financial support from the Basque Government.

Library of Congress Cataloging-in-Publication Data

Uranga, Mikel Gómez, 1948–
    Basque economy: from industrialization to globalization / Mikel Gómez Uranga, Xabier Barrutia, Anton Borja; translated into English by Ana Olabe.
    p. ; cm. — (Basque textbooks series)
  Includes bibliographical references and index.
  ISBN 1-877802-10-7 (paperback)
  ISBN 1-877802-11-5 (hardcover)
  ISBN 1-877802-12-3 (compact disk)
  1. País Vasco (Spain)—Economic conditions. 2. País Vasco (Spain)—Economic policy. 3. Pays Basque (France)—Economic conditions. 4. Pays Basque (France)—Economic policy. I. Barrutia, Xabier, 1966- II. Borja, Anton. III. Title. IV. Series.

  N3412.4 .Z85 2002
  307.3'416'094663090511--dc21
                                      2002014096

Published by the Center for Basque Studies
University of Nevada, Reno /322
Reno, Nevada 89557-0012.

Copyright ©2003 by the Center for Basque Studies.
All rights reserved.

Printed in the United States of America.

CONTENTS

1 · Basque institutions of the Ancien Régime 7
2 · Industrialization in the Basque Country 18
3 · The Basque economy in the Franco era 26
4 · Expansion in the 1960s and 1970s, part I 34
5 · Expansion in the 1960s and 1970s, part II 42
6 · Deindustrialization 1973–85 49
7 · Economic indicators: mid-1970s to mid-1980s .. 56
8 · Development of Basque institutions 63
9 · Basque economy and globalization 72
10 · Jurisdiction 82
11 · Service industry in the Southern Basque Country 91
12 · Infrastructures 98
13 · Geography and infrastructure 107
14 · Agriculture 118
15 · The Basque fishing sector 128
16 · Geography of industry 136
17 · Technology and innovation policy 144
18 · Industry, innovation, perspectives 154
19 · Relationships of innovation 164
20 · Cooperatives and the social economy 172
21 · The Mondragón cooperative system 182
22 · Social welfare coverage 190
23 · The financial sector 201
24 · Current economic indicators 211
25 · Metropolitan areas, part I 219
26 · Metropolitan areas, part II 229
27 · Northern Basque Country, part I 238
28 · Northern Basque Country, part II 246
    List of abbreviations 253
    Endnotes 254
    Picture credits 257
    Index 258
    Colophon 278

1 · Basque institutions
The Ancien Régime and the liberal revolution

WITHIN THE EUROPE of the Ancien Régime towards the mideighteenth century, Basque society had its own distinct characteristics in both the Northern (Labourd, Soule, and Basse Navarre) and the Southern (Araba, Bizkaia, Gipuzkoa, and Navarre) Basque Country.[1] Apart from certain features unique to each historic territory, all shared several predominant features: The majority of the population was made up of peasants living on farms. The farm was the basic unit of social life and production; its near self-sufficiency was common throughout the Basque territories. Each farm comprised a detached house with a long-standing tradition and even a name (which was kept when the farm changed owner) and around 4 to 8 hectares of property made up of small plots of land that were used for household consumption and of forest.

Farms were generally self-sufficient with regard to foodstuffs, except for wheat and, occasionally, meat and wine. This deficiency, however, was compensated for by cash income connected predominantly with steel activities and foral free trade.

The relative stability of the farm sector depended on several factors: continuation of the family line, maintenance of an undivided farm, and relative self-suffiency in food production (partially helped by wine- and linen-making). Artisanship spread widely throughout the Basque Country, often becoming a complementary activity for peasants. Nonetheless, in the eighteenth century money was frequently necessary for both buying complementary foodstuffs and paying rents.

The nearby mountains were very important for the peasant population. They provided lime, wood, and fern;

Mining property belonged to the villages, and the ore to those who extracted it.
Engraving from Harold Hart: The Illustrator's Handbook.

---

pasture for cattle and sheep; and charcoal and iron ore (sources of income). In the traditional system of the Ancien Régime, mountains and woods were open to free exploitation by all residents, as either communal land or the property of the municipality or village.

THIS SYSTEM WAS tenuous, however. Any natural disaster caused subsistance crisis, due to the narrow margins of the population's subsistence and production.

The production sector as a whole was governed by a number of regulations and institutions, which varied throughout the Basque Country. In the Southern Basque

Country, the foral system determined the relationship between private property and collective use of the land. Common property, from which villagers benefited freely and directly, was distinguished from private property, the use of which was reserved for the municipality. Circulation of livestock was regulated. Mining property belonged to the villages, and the ore belonged to those who extracted it. Legislation of these matters was thorough and precise.

The foral system, moreover, had customs legislation advantageous for the population in subsistence matters. Wheat, sparse in Bizkaia and Gipuzkoa, entered freely by sea, much more cheaply than it would have on the southern, overland route (through the customs with Castile).

INSTITUTIONAL SYSTEM OF THE FORAL TERRORITIES
Throughout the medieval and modern ages, the territories that currently form the Basque Country always retained a marked cultural and political character that made them different from the surrounding territories. A number of factors resulted in various sociospatial networks of power following different models and degrees. Among them, Navarre, being a kingdom, was the highest in rank. The political units were characterized by a plural legal-institutional framework and by a wide dispersion of the spheres of power and law: the towns, *señoríos* (manor houses), the church, *corporaciones* (trade associations), and lastly, the crown (represented by a *virrey*, a substitute of the king; a *corregidor*, a kind of governor; or otherwise, depending on the territory).

A system of assemblies and corporative committees constituted the institutional network of the foral system, from the local bases to the summit of the central institutions of each territory.

On a local basis, decisions were made in assemblies around the parish (in Soule) or through representatives elected in towns, villages, parishes, or brotherhoods. The mechanics of representation to intermediate (territorial) and central institutions gradually became more remote, and the Juntas Generales (general assemblies) and deputations (or councils) increased their importance.

Disputes among institutions were resolved, following appeal, by the Juntas Generales. Disputes of private interest, by contrast, went to court.

ECONOMIC DEVELOPMENT IN THE ANCIEN RÉGIME
Forests covered large areas of the country in the Northern Basque Country. Agriculture, pasture rents, and livestock were the main economic resources. The socioeconomic framework of Labourd, Basse Navarre, and Soule was completed with iron forging, fishing in the Basque ports, very active trade in the port of Bayonne (the chamber of commerce was founded in 1726), and the industries and artisanship that subsequently arose.

The eighteenth century witnessed an increase of cultivation area (ploughing lands) within the agricultural sector and stagnation of livestock breeding in the Northern Basque Country.

IRON PRODUCTION (in forges) increased, due to a resurgence of international demand, the strengthening of the Castilian market, the growth of American colonial demand, the reinforcement of protectionist shipbuilding laws, and the rise of some emerging industries (copper, textiles, flour).

Trade became a basic sector because of increased production and commercialization of steel products as well as the boom of intermediate activities (reexporting other companies' goods). The port of Bilbao was an intermediary center for the redistribution of goods throughout Europe. San Sebastián, where the Real Compañía Guipuzcoana de Caracas rose to prominence, was the other major commercial center.

THE ECONOMIC situation worsened during the last quarter of the century. Expansion in the agricultural sector was blocked. The Basque steel industry entered a recession, due partly to the inability to compete technologically in foreign markets and partly to the crown's willingness to import foreign iron. Trade also decreased because American colonial independence gave rise to liberalization. Basque ports were excluded from this process, to the advantage of other Spanish ports.

NORTHERN BASQUE COUNTRY

The French Revolution in 1789 dismantled the existing institutional framework, including its conception of private and public rights. The elimination of both birthright laws and the collective use of common lands went against the interests and traditions of the Basque territories.

The liberal principles of economic freedom and individual private property were soon felt. At the beginning of the nineteenth century, the use rights to forests and common fields (free passing of livestock, tree fellage) were eliminated, although some of these rights were partially restored as a result of peasant opposition.

Traditional agriculture continued, and small landholders exploited their own land at a rate of 80%. Artisanship encouraged industrial progress and the liberalization of trade. Shoemaking became industrialized to a degree in Mauleon and Hasparren. Industrial building decreased in Bayonne, but the Forjas del Adour was founded in 1881; afterwards, a cement factory and a factory of railway lines provided the port with some industrial activity. The Paris-Bordeaux railway line was built in 1855 and extended first to Bayonne and then, in 1864, to Irun.

WITH REGARD to commerce, since 1814 Bayonne argued repeatedly but in vain for the restoration of the 1784 customs exemption and the transfer of French customs to north of the Adour River. Trade with the Spanish state continued to decline, however, except during the two Carlist Wars (1833–39 and 1872–76), when trade between Bayonne and the Northern Iberian Peninsula flourished.

Tourism was already important in the midnineteenth century. The new railway to Biarritz attracted the court, high administration, and distinguished foreign visitors to the Basque coast. At the beginning of the twentieth century, the coast became overcrowded with tourists from all over Europe.

The population grew from 126,493 inhabitants in 1801 to 167,317 in 1881. In the midnineteenth century, a series of agricultural crises combined with industrial stagnation to bring increased debt and the impoverishment of rural markets. The result was an exodus to larger towns and cities and to America. At the end of the nineteenth century and the beginning of the twentieth, increased population density, especially on the coast, was accompanied by a major trend towards depopulation of the inland areas of the Northern Basque Country.

SOUTHERN BASQUE COUNTRY

The two Carlist Wars (1833–39 and 1872–76) were the violent expression of the collapse of the Ancien Régime.

The transition from the Ancien Régime to a bourgeois liberal society meant the definitive disappearence of feudalism and the adoption of a model of social organization inspired by liberal principles.

High society
The new railway to Biarritz attracted the court, high administration, and distinguished foreign visitors to the Basque coast.
Engraving: Punch.

This transition covered the period between the last third of the e¡ighteenth century and the second half of the nineteenth century, although some historians extend it to as late as 1876.

The bourgeois liberal regime was based on the following ideas: legal equality and the elimination of tax and feudal privileges; a constitutional-liberal political system; institutional-political and economic unity of the monarchy. It entailed the application of a centralizing strategy on the part of a state with a uniformist creed.

Consequently, the traditional foral regime disappeared, and the Southern Basque Country was integrated into a unified Spanish market. Customs borders were eliminated between the Southern Basque Country on one hand and Castile and Aragón on the other. Lastly, liberalization of property and agricultural restructuring caused the abolishment of *señoríos* and feudal property, and the rights of the *señorío* and the tithe, and resulted in the sale of civil and church property and price liberalization.

This transition occurred during a serious economic crisis marked by social tension that was extreme and sometimes violent (the Carlist Wars). The traditional system's intrinsic limitations played an essential role in this crisis. During the first half of the nineteenth century, a phase of diminishing gross agricultural product was accompanied by a tendency toward price depression until 1833. A significant decrease in income affected the Basque farming classes: direct producers, tenant farmers, small *jauntxos* (rent-receiving lords that sold their own crops), and large landowners. As many peasants could not pay the tithe owed the church, the agricultural crisis affected the low clergy as well.

THE INCREASING sense of alienation that accompanied the sale of both civil and church property was particularly marked in the Southern Basque Country. Until the first third of the nineteenth century, such sales affected municipal property. Much church property was confiscated in Navarre, where that institution was rich in real estate. Between 1835 and 1876, this activity extended throughout Navarre and Araba and, to a lesser extent (due to the comparative dearth of church properties), Bizkaia and Gipuzkoa. It did not generally enable tenants and farm workers to acquire property, but favored property concentration.

Table 1-1.
Evolution of the population

	Bizkaia	**Gipuzkoa**	**Araba**	**Navarre**
1787	116,042	120,716	71,399	227,382
1797	111,603	104,491	69,158	NA
1810	112,920	115,587	70,000	NA
1825	144,875	135,838	92,807	NA
1857	160,579	156,493	96,398	299,654

NA = *not available.*
Source: *Great Historical Atlas of the Basque World*

The difficulties were severe enough to cause the population to level off. There was a deceleration in population increase until the first Carlist War. The conjunction of population growth and economic crisis was directly connected to migration and poverty. The evolution of the population is shown in Table 1-1.

Traditional industry also fared poorly. Shipbuilding declined, iron production diminished as a result of falling exports (due to Swedish competition), and the internal market of the Spanish crown (including its possessions) was decreasing. International trade was also in crisis. The Compañía de Caracas disappeared.

INTERNATIONAL EVENTS worsened the situation. The Convention Wars (1793–95) and the Napoleonic Wars (1808–14), along with the riots in 1821 and the Carlist Wars, brought turmoil and debt, especially for the town councils, which were obliged to auction off common lands in order to make their payments. Liberal principles were already in evidence at that time. In 1825, the General Law of Mines, liberal in spirit (albeit with certain limitations), was passed.

The Carlist Wars were the incarnation of the crisis of the Ancien Régime that brought the least bloodshed. Their inspiration was purportedly the question of succession rights to the throne. In reality, the Carlist revolt in the Basque Country was spearheaded by several distinct social movements. Carlism brought about a popular rebellion, mainly of peasants, but also consisting of the urban lower classes, and antiliberal small rural lords and clergy.

Several segments of the population joined to support the new liberal regime in expectation of potential benefits: the rural oligarchy and a segment of the landowning aristocracy; urban, merchant, and industrial bourgeoisie; civil servants and liberal professionals; a minority among the high clergy; and some minority sectors among the lower classes.

Some of the fallout of the two Carlist Wars merits mention: the Ley Paccionada (Pacted Law) of 1841 entirely dismantled the foral system in Navarre in practice; similarly, the Decree of Espartero (1841) moved the borders to Irun, abolished foral free trade, and brought the Juntas Generales to their end.

THE LAW ABOLISHING the foral system was declared in 1876. Basque bourgeois liberalism thus achieved its economic goals with the institution of the Concierto Económico, an economic agreement that determined a special system of tax allocation between Bizkaia, Gipuzkoa, and Araba on one hand and the Spanish state on the other. The Concierto Económico established that each territory would contribute to the state treasury in accordance with its wealth.

17 · Basque institutions

Lesson one

SUGGESTED READING
Kurlansky, M. *The Basque History of the World*. New York: Walker and Company. Chapters 6, 7, and 8.

BIBLIOGRAPHY
Agirreazkuenaga, J. (Dir). *Gran atlas histórico del mundo vasco.* 1994. Bilbao: El Mundo del País Vasco.
Harrison, J. 1977. "Big Business and the Rise of Basque Nationalism." *European Studies Review*, no. 4.
Kurlansky, M. 1999. *The Basque History of the World.* New York: Walker and Company.

LEARNING GOALS
1. Identify the main institutional elements of the Basque provinces within the context of the Ancien Régime.
2. Describe the main aspects of economic development in the eighteenth and nineteenth centuries.

WRITTEN LESSON FOR SUBMISSION
1. Describe the main features of the foral, economic, and institutional system.
2. What were the most critical factors provoking the crisis of the foral system? Describe the differences between the Northern and Southern Basque Country.

2 · Industrialization in the Basque Country

ECONOMIC MODERNIZATION in the Basque Country has its roots in the double revolution (political and economic) brought about in modern times. The French political revolution introduced liberal ideas and the need to model the state into a nation-state. The English industrial revolution promoted the development of capitalism and a new industrial society.

The construction of the Spanish and French markets and the industrialization of the Basque Country occurred within that historical framework. Basque economic development, however, is also the result of its own contemporary history: a dynamic commercial bourgeoisie; a long-standing tradition in shipbuilding and steelworks with a qualified workforce; and an abundance of iron ore, the valuable raw material for the modern steel industry.

Industrial Modernization (1839–1900)
THE NORTHERN BASQUE COUNTRY
Industrialization was relatively important in the Northern Basque Country. In the second half of the nineteenth century the railway was extended to Bayonne (1854) and Hendaye (1864). But despite the emergence of certain industries—such as footwear in Hasparren, sandal-making in Mauleon, and furnaces installed in Boucou in 1833—agriculture and livestock breeding remained the dominant activities. On the other hand, tourism became important beginning in the midnineteenth century, as evidenced by the population growth in Biarritz (from 2,048 inhabitants in 1851 to 18,260 in 1911).

Trade was fostered through the port of Bayonne, by exports of iron, coal, and other goods, as well as steel and rails.

As a consequence of the agricultural crises and industrial problems of the midnineteenth century, waves of emigrants headed for America. Between 1832 and 1884, 64,227 people left Bayonne.

In conclusion, the industrial model of the Northern Basque Country was weak, due to dependence on agriculture based on small landed property and capital, trade, and services.

THE SOUTHERN BASQUE COUNTRY
Industrialization in the Southern Basque Country has its origins in the period 1841–72.

AFTER THE FIRST Carlist War, the triumph of liberal ideas, integration of the Basque territories into the newly institutionalizing Spanish state, and withdrawal of customs from the interior to the coast combined with the advent of capitalism to usher in a new era. The modern steel industry was founded, as were paper and textiles, modern iron-mining operations, shipbuilding, the banking sector, the weapons and metal industry, and railways.

In the mining sector, the so-called mining concessions were instituted as a result of the Mining Laws of 1825, thus giving way to the system of free private property. The new Mining Laws of 1859 enabled the exploitation of mines on a larger scale, due to the expectations created by the Bessemer method (discovered in 1855 and applied to nonphosphoric iron ore) for extracting steel. To promote the export of iron ore from Bizkaia, the deputation paid for the construction of the railway that connected the mining zone of Somorrostro with the coast in 1865. During those years, seven foreign mining companies were founded (six of them English). The quantity of ore extracted increased from 70,000 metric tons in 1860 to 250,000 in 1870. Great Britain became the most important client, and the ships brought back freights of coal, thereby contributing to the consolidation of a more modern steel industry. As late as 1880, out of the 2,684,000 metric tons extracted, only 71,000 were used in Bizkaian steel mills. Over 90% of the ore extracted was therefore exported, with England the leading destination. The 1890s were the peak years, with an average of four million metric tons mined per year.

In the organization of the mining business, the owners belonged to a Basque elite, and the exploiting companies were owned by both foreigners and Basques. The mining business energized the railway and ship companies, whose freight accounted for between 35% and 45% of the final price of iron.

THE ESTIMATED total worth of the material for the period 1876–1900 was 1 billion pesetas, a spectacular sum in those days.

The need to transport iron ore promoted the construction of new cargo ships. The metric tonnage of the cargo fleet registered in Bilbao went from 65,775 in 1882 to 305,000 in 1900. Eminent members of the mining bourgeoisie (such as Sota y Aznar and Gandarias) also became leading shipowners.

During the period between the Carlist Wars, Nuestra Señora de la Merced (1846) and Nuestra Señora del Carmen (1855), two new steel mills considered pioneers of the modern steel industry, were founded.

Several factors contributed to the construction of the San Francisco de Mudela, La Vizcaya, and the Altos Hornos de Bilbao (AHB) steel mills: the convergence of capital in space (the river mouth of Bilbao) and time (the 1870s and 1880s), iron ore, adequate technology,

Growth of the armaments sector
Industrialization in Gipuzkoa was characterized by a greater diversity than in Bizkaia. Weapons production grew markedly during the last decade of the nineteenth century and the beginning of the twentieth century. *Engraving from Heck's* Pictorial Archive of Military Science, Geography, and History.

---

and internal and external iron markets. These three mills combined to produce 80% of Spanish iron and steel during the 1880s. In 1902, Altos Hornos de Vizcaya was founded through the merger of AHB, La Vizcaya, and La Iberia. In 1912, sales totalled 60 million pesetas, the highest for any company in the Basque economy.

WITH RESPECT TO the banking sector, Banco de Bilbao was founded in 1856 with 2 million pesetas in capital; Banco de San Sebastián in 1862 with 1 million; and Banco de Comercio in 1891 with 4 million pesetas of disbursed capital. In the nineteenth century, Basque banks experienced constant growth, providing credit to

Table 2-1:
Population of the Southern Basque Country (1857–1900)

	Bizkaia	Gipuzkoa	Araba	Navarre
1857	160,579	156,493	96,398	299,654
1877	189,954	167,207	93,191	304,184
1887	235,659	181,845	92,915	304,122
1900	311,361	195,850	96,385	303,669

Source: *Great Historical Atlas of the Basque World*.

the most successful mining sectors and to the steel and other industries.

Industrialization in Gipuzkoa was characterized by greater decentralization and sectorial diversity than in Bizkaia. During the 1860s, investments were made in the paper and textiles sector and in the steel sector. Weapons production grew markedly during the last decade of the nineteenth century and the first two decades of the twentieth. Industrialization was secondary to agriculture in Araba and Navarre (glossing over the differences between these two territories). In 1900, agriculture accounted for 60% and 70% of the active population in Araba and Navarre, with a mere 15% and 11%, respectively, involved in industry.

The evolution of the population by territory is shown in Table 2-1.

THE GREATEST increase in population took place in Bizkaia and Gipuzkoa, whereas Araba and Navarre were stagnant. In 1900, 82,000 of Bizkaia's inhabitants—26% of the total—came from other provinces, with one quarter of such migrants coming from other Basque territories.

THE EVOLUTION IN PRODUCTION (1900–1936)
During the first third of the twentieth century, the already established Basque bourgeoisie expanded and consolidated its areas of influence through a network of mines, steel, ships, and finance. At the turn of the century, Bizkaia had more factories than any other province in the state, including twenty-seven large steel mills and shipbuilders, sixty-seven factories and metal workshops, seventeen shipowning companies, and various factories for paper, flour, electricity, and canned foodstuffs.

The mining sector, especially exports, stagnated from 1914 to 1936. The steel sector, however, continued its expansion through the century's first two decades, although its production would subsequently decline. Two factors had positive effects on industry. One was a 1926 law protecting industries, which reinforced traditional Spanish tariff protectionism. The other was the measures promoting public works and the railway, enforced from 1926 through 1931, during the dictatorship of General Primo de Rivera. The effects of this conjuncture were especially salient in Bizkaia, which achieved the highest production rates in its history in 1929 (424,979 metric tons of iron and 536,766 metric tons of steel). During the republican period (1931–36), the level of production fell sharply because the decrease in the construction of public works brought crisis.

CLOSELY LINKED to exports of iron ore and its by-products, the shipbuilding sector experienced unprecedented growth during the first two decades of the twentieth century. Euskalduna was founded in 1900, the Sociedad Española de Construcción Naval in 1915. One consequence of the 1929 crisis was a decline in sea traffic, which directly affected the shipbuilding sector.

The situation was very positive for the banking business, however. In 1901, Banco de Vizcaya was founded.

Table 2-2:
Population of the Southern Basque Country (1900–1940).

	Bizkaia	Gipuzkoa	Araba	Navarre
1900	311,361	195,850	96,385	303,669
1910	349,923	226,684	97,181	312,235
1920	409,550	258,557	98,668	329,875
1930	485,205	302,329	104,176	345,883
1940	511,135	331,753	112,876	369,618

Source: R. G. Alvarez Llano (1997).

It and Banco de Bilbao would be the two leading banks of the Spanish finance oligarchy. Some other, less important banks, such as Banco Guipuzcoano, Banco de San Sebastián, Banco de Tolosa, and Banco de Vitoria, also appeared. Banking flourished due not only to economic development but also to Spain's neutrality in World War I.

The already mentioned dynamics of production influenced the evolution of population in the four territories. As Table 2-2 shows, the largest population increase between 1900 and 1940 occurred in Bizkaia (almost 200,000) and in Gipuzkoa (136,000).

WITH RESPECT to the number of immigrants, in 1920, 46% of them settled in Gipuzkoa; 35% of immigrants to Araba, 22% of those to Bizkaia, and 20% of those to Navarre came from other parts of the Basque Country. It also merits mention that, in 1920, 31,000 Gipuzkoan res- idents (12% of its total population) and 88,586 of those in Bizkaia (22% of its total population) were immigrants from other Spanish provinces.

Lesson two

BIBLIOGRAPHY
Agirreazkuenaga, J. (Dir). Gran atlas histórico del mundo vasco. 1994. Bilbao: El Mundo del País Vasco.

LEARNING GOAL
Describe the main aspects of industrial modernization during the second half of the nineteenth century and first half of the twentieth century.

WRITTEN LESSON FOR SUBMISSION
1. Explain the main differences in industrial modernization between the Northern and Southern Basque Country.
2. Clarify the main demographic implications of the model of industrialization developed in the Southern Basque Country during the second half of the nineteenth century and first half of the twentieth century.

3 · Basque economy in the Franco era

THE SITUATION of Basque industry during the 1940s was problematic, especially because of the shortage of supplies caused by both autarkic home policies and the effects of the European war. Almost all sectors of Basque industry stagnated due to inadaptability and the lack of basic supplies (raw materials, coal, electric energy, and so on).

The shortage of coal and tin affected the steel industry overall (factories worked below their production capacity). As these materials were vital to the steel sector, their shortage had devastating consequences for individual companies (as in the case of Babcock Wilcox, Talleres Euskalduna, CAF, and so on). This was also the case in other sectors. As paper factories could not obtain the usual Scandinavian paper paste, they had to resort to homemade supplies. Chemical factories and rubber makers could not import the necessary raw materials; as a result, several factories (including Firestone and Vidrieras de Llodio) had to discontinue or reduce production for several months.

This lack of materials encouraged the creation of Basque companies whose goal was to compensate for such shortages, such as Acerías y Forjas de Azkoitia (1939), Aceros de Llodio (1940), Esteban Orbegozo (1944), and Aristrain (1956), among others. Unquinesa (1939) was founded in Bizkaia to supply coal to AHV (Altos Hornos de Vizcaya); Sefanitro (1941) was created to produce parts for the AHV furnaces. Nonetheless, the economic situation began to improve, especially during the 1950s. The industrial census listed 4,698 companies in 1955; out of these, 414 (with 47.9 million pesetas in capital) were created that very year.

27 · Basque economy in the Franco era

In 1942, industrial activity in Araba and Navarre was less important than in the other two Southern Basque territories. In Araba, there were fifty-seven woodworking shops, about the same number of saw mills and carpenter shops, some flour factories, and two metal factories. In 1955, the industrial census listed 1,624 companies, mainly small, with under five million pesetas in capital in the case of the recent ones.

Industries for the transformation of farm products were significant in Navarre. There were sixty-one factories for flour, three apiece for beets and canned vegetables, and two for fertilizer.

During the 1940s and 1950s, iron ore extraction slowed, due partly to a labor shortage and partly to the decline in the export market resulting from high prices. In 1949, mining production in Bizkaia was 750,000 metric tons, of which 244,000 were exported. In 1958, production in Bizkaia rose to 1,322,000 metric tons from eighty-five mines of varying importance. Only three produced more than 100,000 metric tons. Nevertheless, in 1963, with a sharp fall in production and exports, mining's heyday was over.

During the 1940s, the steel industry, shipbuilding, transformed metal goods, and chemicals were the sectors that spearheaded the industrial resurgence.

DESPITE THE restrictions on raw materials, the Bizkaian steel industry became very important within Spain (over 50% of state production). Among the companies that stand out during the Spanish postwar years, Altos Hornos de Vizcaya in particular merits mention, especially after its 1939 takeover of Siderurgia del Mediterráneo. In 1942, Altos Hornos de Vizcaya had 250 million pesetas of capital and a production capacity of 700,000 metric tons of iron ingots and quite a bit more

The shipbuilding sector
Workers at the Euskalduna and La Naval shipyards built between eighteen and twenty-eight midsize ships per year throughout the 1950s.
Engraving from Johann George Heck: The Complete Encyclopedia of Illustration.

---

of steel. Table 3-1 shows iron and steel production in Bizkaia from 1940 to 1950.

IN THE SHIPBUILDING sector, seventy-seven ships were built between the years 1941 and 1949 with a total tonnage of 34,400. In the 1950s, between eight (in 1955) and twenty (in 1959) ships were built by the builders of

Table 3-1
Steel production in Bizkaia (in metric tons)

	Iron ingots	Steel	Steel sheets
1940	423,482	477,499	472,857
1945	283,206	312,626	186,988
1950	366,428	418,747	248,077

Source: García Crespo et al. (1981).

large ships (Euskalduna and La Naval); these companies built between eighteen and twenty-eight midsize ships per year throughout that decade. Fishing boat construction (done by other companies) averaged twenty-five per year until 1956, increasing to forty-five in 1959.

The chemical sector was made up of two hundred companies with more than 12,000 workers in Bizkaia in 1950. In Gipuzkoa, fifty-five companies with 1,940 workers were registered.

The machine-tool industry evolved from its pre-1940 beginnings to become relatively significant in the 1940s and 1950s. From 1940 to 1950, twenty-five new companies started making machine tools, and between 1950 and 1959 another fifty-six began operations.

BUSINESS DYNAMISM is evident in the number of new companies created between 1940 and 1950: 1,253, with a total registered capital of 1.937 billion pesetas.

A natural reflection of this productive dynamism and inflow of income is also observable in the evolution of banks, especially Banco de Bilbao and Banco de Vizcaya. Banco de Bilbao's profits during the period 1936–50 were 503.3 million pesetas; Banco de Vizcaya's 519.1

Table 3-2.
Evolution of the population

	Bizkaia	**Gipuzkoa**	**Araba**	**Navarre**
1940	511,135	331,753	112,876	369,618
1950	569,188	374,040	118,012	382,932
1960	751,014	478,337	138,934	402,042

Source: *Great Historical Atlas of the Basque Country.*

million pesetas. Banking activity was also reflected in the volume of transactions on the stock exchange in Bilbao: 0.57 billion pesetas from 1941 to 1946.

During the 1940s, labor relations were marked by an increasing interventionism. The state, consistent with the Franco government's fascist creed, controlled both prices and wages. Several reports on postwar wages show a clear trend toward a declining worker standard of living. The situation was the result of both decreasing productivity and greater exploitation of the workforce. Workers were forced to work extras hours in order to increase their purchasing power, with overtime becoming a substantial part of their income. On the whole, however, consumption did not return to Civil War levels.

ON THE OTHER hand, due to the shortage of consumer goods (foodstuffs, clothes, domestic equipment), prices shot up. Although Franco's government tried to control prices, a black market emerged, coexisting with the official market in the provision of those goods. By way of comparison, taking an index of 100 in 1936 as a basis, wages reached an average value of 130, while official prices went up to 593, and prices in the black market reached a value of 1,033.

During the 1950s, Pamplona and Vitoria-Gasteiz underwent industrialization. In Vitoria-Gasteiz, the role of the Deputation and municipal government was decisive. Both offered already developed sites to companies establishing themselves in the territory. The deputation of Navarre and the municipal government of Pamplona also played a critical role in the foundation of a great number of companies. A group of Navarrese capitalists (including Huarte and Huici) were protagonists, founding such companies as Sarrió, Potasas de Navarra, Agni, and Laminaciones de Lesaca.

IN SHORT, the financial concentration of the times was unprecedented. Protectionism, acute inflation, repression of the working class, and development of the banking sector all combined to promote new iron, machinery, and chemical companies in the Southern Basque Country. Many of these companies, however, did not have the technical know-how or productive capacity necessary.

The overall yearly GDP (gross domestic product) of the Southern Basque Country rose from 4.143 billion pesetas to 17.706 billion pesetas between 1940 and 1950—an increase above the Spanish average. During the 1940s, Bizkaia was the territory that developed most quickly, followed by Gipuzkoa (both exceeded the state average); Navarre and Araba both fell below the Spanish average.

The GDP of the Southern Basque Country totalled 51.61 billion pesetas in 1960. During the 1950s Bizkaia was also the most dynamic of the territories, experiencing above average growth, followed by Gipuzkoa and Navarre.

The Basque banking sector played a highly significant role in this economic development through its influence on industry. Banco de Bilbao and Banco de Vizcaya moved capital and decisively influenced companies in all sectors: electric, steel, shipbuilding, chemicals, foodstuffs, transportation, construction, and shipping.

During the 1940s and 1950s, exports from the Southern Basque Country were low. With the exception of Navarre, which actively participated in the export of farming products, foreign sales were significant only in iron ore. In 1951, significant export of manufactured goods began, ranging between 500 and 800 million pesetas worth per year during the 1950s. Of the territories, this activity was virtually exclusive to Bizkaia and Gipuzkoa, since industrialization did not take place until the 1950s in Araba and the 1960s in Navarre.

DURING THE 1950s, worker purchasing power improved somewhat as a result of increasing wages, but it remained too low to cover basic necessities. The black market and ration books disappeared, and the normal provision of basic necessities was restored.

As a result of worker demonstrations in 1956, the government was compelled to increase wages, further contributing to the already existing inflationary process.

On the other hand, although net wages in 1958 were still below the 1936 level, the significant increase in production had a positive effect on economic surplus and capital profitability.

The evolution of the population is shown in Table 3-2.

Considering migration among Basque territories and natural population growth, immigration to the Basque Country during the 1950s was particularly significant in Bizkaia and Gipuzkoa and, to a much lesser degree, in Araba.

Lesson three

BIBLIOGRAPHY

Agirreazkuenaga, J. (Dir). *Gran atlas histórico del mundo vasco*. 1994. Bilbao: El Mundo del País Vasco.

Garcia Crespo, M., et al. 1981. "La economía vasca durante el franquismo: crecimiento y crisis de la economía vasca, 1936–1980." *Gran Enciclopedia Vasca*. Bilbao.

LEARNING GOAL

Describe the main aspects of the Basque economy in Franco's time, from 1940 to 1960.

WRITTEN LESSON FOR SUBMISSION

1. Distinguish the distinct features in the economic development of the four territories Araba, Gipuzkoa, Bizkaia, and Navarre.
2. Was the demographic dynamic similar in all these territories? Explain the most important aspects.

4 · Expansion in the 1960s and 1970s
Part I

THE PROCESS of capitalist economic development in the Southern Basque Country in the early 1960s was conditioned primarily by the evolution of capital accumulation in the Spanish state. The intensive phase of capital development, characterized by a rise in mass consumption, brought about a growth of the subsector of nonperishable consumer goods (electrical appliances, automobiles, consumer electronics, housing), of final transformed chemicals, and of some final components of traditional common consumer goods.

As a result of its idiosyncratic historical development, the Basque economy had been highly specialized in intermediate and final production means (steel, cement, machinery). In the 1960s, it received a tremendous boost in the expansion of new mass consumer goods. The boom in the manufacturing of electrical appliances, automobiles, plastic goods, and other such products stemmed from the need to provide intermediate steel, metal, and chemical inputs, as well as machinery and capital goods in order to cover an increasing demand for consumer goods. In addition, the various subsectors of production (machinery, steel, and so on) had ever growing demands due to their own productive processes.

In this period the profit margin of the productive sector in Bizkaia, Gipuzkoa, and Araba rose at an annual average rate of 3.5%. This is due to the fact that the increase in work productivity surpassed that in salaries. The evolution of the Southern Basque Country's GDP is shown in Table 4-1.

The sheer increase of GDP in Bizkaia and Gipuzkoa is remarkable. This trend was particularly noteworthy between 1960 and 1971, when the biannual GDP

Table 4-1.
Basque GDP (billion pesetas, constant)

	1960	1967	1971	1975
Araba	12.867	27.678	41.131	50.751
Gipuzkoa	60.866	92.197	123.844	143.895
Navarre	33.385	55.388	71.912	85.655
Bizkaia	87.912	148.501	188.080	246.357
Total	195.030	323.764	424.967	526.658

Source: Banco de Bilbao.

increase in the Southern Basque Country ranged between 11.4% and 24.7%.

THE DEVELOPMENT of wealth was not homogeneous by sector. In the agricultural sector of Bizkaia, Gipuzkoa, and Araba, the added value (constant pesetas) decreased from 12.3% of the total (1955) to 8.8% (1964) to 5.1% (1975). The trend differed in Navarre, where agriculture accounted for 33% of the GDP in 1960 but decreased to 16.7% in 1973. In the industrial sector in Bizkaia, Gipuzkoa, and Araba, the added value (in constant pesetas) went from 51.8% (1955) to 57.2% (1964) to 63.7% (1975). The development of the industrial sector in Navarre went from 32.7% of the GDP in 1960 to 41.8% in 1973. Lastly, during the 1960s and 1970s, the service sector became increasingly more important in both Bizkaia, Gipuzkoa, and Araba on the one hand (31.2% of their gross added value in 1975) and Navarre on the other (41.5% of the GDP in 1973).

Development Plan I was created in 1964 to cover the next four years. The Deputation of Navarre created a Plan of Industrial Promotion for development in the Pamplona area. Nevertheless, among the objectives was to balance the distribution of industrial expansion in order to avoid capital concentration. The promotional strategy was also designed to mobilize savings and autonomous financial resources and to attract foreign capital. These and other objectives constituted a program that turned out to be very influential in the configuration of Navarrese industry.

Notwithstanding, the Southern Basque Country remained outside the strategy schemes implemented by the development plans.

PUBLIC AND PRIVATE INVESTMENT

Between 1971 and 1975, private investment totalled 71.8 billion pesetas, accounting for between 16% and 22% of that in Spain. Investment in machinery represented 70% of the total in fixed assets, and the sectors of metal goods and chemicals absorbed the greatest amounts of money.

As a result of the new liberalization measures in 1959 dealing with the entry of capital, foreign investment was to be decisive in certain sectors. Between 1960 and 1972, direct majoritarian foreign investment in the Southern Basque Country is estimated to have been 7.18 billion pesetas—10% of the total foreign investment in the entire state. In 1974, 6.6% of the companies in Bizkaia had foreign capital, and 25% of all capital was foreign. Chemicals was the sector with the highest foreign participation, followed by transformed metal goods.

By country of origin, the United States and Switzerland accounted for 80% of the total foreign investment from 1966 to 1971, while France was the leading investor from 1975 to 1977.

The sectors in which foreign capital was most active between 1966 and 1971 were chemicals (69% of foreign

Sanctions at the outset
Francisco Franco's government seems to have been clearly bent on discriminating against Bizkaia and Gipuzkoa, which were officially designated "traitor provinces."

---

investment) and steel (22%). From 1975 through 1977, chemicals remained first, followed closely by foodstuffs (mainly in Navarre) and capital goods.

IN TERMS OF public investment, some relevant aspects of the participation of the state in the Basque economy will now be addressed. In the post–Civil War years, Franco's government seems to have been clearly bent on discriminating against the Southern Basque Country economically—especially Bizkaia and Gipuzkoa, officially designated "traitor provinces." This is evident in the rejection of a great number of the applications that had been made to the Ministry of Industry to create or expand associations.

As a consequence, the National Institute of Industry (INI), a state company created in 1941, was largely inactive in the Basque economy; in fact, its only real contribution in the Southern Basque Country was the creation of Potasas de Navarra. In 1969, Astilleros Españoles S.A. (AESA) was founded as the result of the merger of La Naval, Euskalduna, and Astilleros de Cádiz, with INI holding a 50% share.

In 1976, INI activity in the Southern Basque Country barely reached 3% of the institute's investment capital—minimal in comparison to its importance in other regions (such as Asturias and Galicia).

THE MOST relevant form of public participation in the Basque economy during the 1960s and 1970s was through joint ventures. The first such joint venture, begun in 1964, surged from seven sectors, including steel and shipbuilding. Ten Basque companies belonging to the comprehensive steel, common steel, and special steel sector participated. Public state loans covered large percentages of the investment made by these companies. The low degree of self-financing of the Basque companies led the state to require that the public loans be replaced by private ones. Repayment would therefore ultimately incur higher debt.

The second joint venture of the noncomprehensive steel industry began in 1974 and lasted until 1982. It established the comprehensive steel industry as "an industry of preferential interest" and included eleven Basque companies. The companies did not freeze investments in spite of the sudden crisis, and debts elevated because of their limited capacity for self-financing.

Within public investment, it is important to highlight the role played by the Foral Deputations, which allocate the resources obtained through tax revenues and the ordinary budget, as well as those acquired through the extraordinary budget and the issuance of securities and loans with financing companies. These institutions make investment of the utmost importance.

THE FIVE-YEAR plan established by the Deputation of Araba for 1971 to 1975 addressed industrial promotion, town planning, and territorial planning. During the next four-year period, 8.5 billion pesetas were invested.

The program of industrial promotion developed by the Foral Deputation of Navarre in 1964–74 mobilized an important volume of resources for economic growth. The results of this program at the end of 1974 can be summed up as follows: 337 companies took part in the plan, with more than 20 billion pesetas in total investment and more than 30,000 new jobs.

THE BASQUE COOPERATIVE MOVEMENT

Ulgor, which made electrical appliances, was founded in Mondragón in 1956. A series of cooperatives soon emerged around it, gradually forming a cooperative cluster. Caja Laboral, the current bank of the cooperative group, was founded in 1959. On one hand, it was quite complicated for the cooperatives to raise enough money for the necessary investment by attracting private investors. On the other, private banks were reluctant to grant loans to worker cooperatives that, anyway, would lose their independence if they went into debt thus.

Since cooperative workers were self-employed and therefore outside the mainstream system of social security, Caja Laboral Popular directed its efforts to the public assistance of the members during those first years.

The Social Provision Service was thereby created; in 1967, it became Lagun-Aro, an independent cooperative.

The growth of the cooperatives has been spectacular. They have diversified into a variety of sectors and expanded services for the group (for example, technological center, techno-professional training).

THE PRESENCE OF FINANCING CAPITAL

The role played by the Basque oligarchy in the state economic and political network from the start of the industrial age onwards enabled Basque capital to become the strongest financial group in Spain. Through Banco de Bilbao and Banco de Vizcaya, Basque capital gained control of hydroelectric companies, shipping companies, paper manufacturers, and other industries in the Spanish state. In 1967, these two banks managed 129.869 billion pesetas and exercised direct control more than fifty-seven companies, with more than 100 million pesetas disbursed.

WITH REGARD to Basque industry, the two banks noted have traditionally participated in and controlled the leading companies in the Basque Country. With the first signs of crisis in the late 1970s, however, there was a withdrawal of financing capital from companies in traditional Basque sectors, such as the steel industry.

By 1975, 594 private bank offices were open in the Southern Basque Country, with deposits totaling 238.731 billion pesetas. With respect to the savings banks, there were 644 branch offices and a total deposit of 172.124 billion pesetas.

The stock exchange, on the other hand, had trading amounting to 5.005 billion pesetas in 1971 and 7.173 billion pesetas in 1975.

41 · Expansion in the 1960s and 1970s, part I

Lesson four

BIBLIOGRAPHY
Fundación BBV. http://www.bbva.es.
University of Mondragón. http://www.muni.es.

LEARNING GOAL
Describe the most important characteristics of the expansive economic development model of the 1960s in the context of Franco's political regime.

WRITTEN LESSON FOR SUBMISSION
1. Identify the features that characterize the structural imbalance (lack of equilibrium) within the Basque industrial framework.
2. What were the respective roles of public and private investments, cooperative movements, and finance capital during these years?

5 · Expansion in the 1960s and 1970s
Part II

BASQUE PRODUCTIVE SPECIALIZATION

DURING THE 1960s and 1970s the relative importance of the Basque agricultural sector diminished, whereas that of the industry and service sectors increased. In 1975, agriculture accounted for 5.7% of the GDP of Bizkaia, Gipuzkoa, and Araba; industry, 47.8%; building, 5.4%; and services, 47.9%. In Navarre, in contrast, the agriculture sector was 17% of the GDP, industry 36.3%, building 5.5%, and services 41.5%.

The development of wealth rates of the different sectors paralleled that of employment. Thus, in Bizkaia, Gipuzkoa, and Araba, agriculture accounted for 17.2% of employment in 1955, 13.2% in 1964, and 8.3% in 1975. Agriculture accounted for 24.8% of total employment in Navarre in 1973.

Industry accounted for 49.9% of employment in Bizkaia, Gipuzkoa, and Araba in 1955, 54.7% in 1964, and 54.6% in 1975. Industry accounted for 43.1% of employment in Navarre in 1973.

Industrial productive specialization in the Southern Basque Country, with the strong presence of the basic metal and transformed metal industries, was further bolstered, influenced by the process of accumulation on a state level. This is because metal manufacturing, in which intermediate goods and investment were clearly predominant, continued to grow within the manufacturing sector as a whole, at the expense of consumer goods.

As shown in Table 5-1, the metal industry increased from 54.2% to 65.2% of the manufacturing industry, to the detriment of the consumer goods sector.

The significance of some Basque industrial subsectors within Spain as a whole is quite marked. The Basque

Table 5-1.
Specialization in manufacturing sectors, Bizkaia, Gipuzkoa, and Araba (%)

	1955	1969	1975
Foodstuffs, drinks, and tobacco	8.2	7.5	5.1
Textiles	5.2	1.3	0.9
Leather, footwear, and clothes	4.2	3.9	2.6
Wood and cork	7.4	3.8	3.2
Press paper and printing	5.7	6.1	6.9
Chemicals	12.8	17.1	13.1
Ceramics and glass	2.2	3.2	3.2
Metal industries	54.2	60.2	65.2
Total of manufacturing industry	100	100	100

Source: *Banco de Bilbao.*

steel industry, for example, accounted for 33% of total Spanish production; 100% of nonwelded tubes; 38% of paper and its by-products; 75% of machine tools; and 66% of tires.

BASQUE PRODUCTION had to maintain close foreign ties to provide markets for surplus goods and access to those in short supply. In 1972, 50% of all production was exported (42% to the Spanish market and 8% to foreign markets).

The main exports were transformed metals (80.58% going abroad); iron and steel (46.38%); manufactured rubber products (88.2%); paper, cardboard, and its transformed products (60.61%); other chemicals (57%); manufactured plastic goods (60.14%); produced and initially transformed noniron metals (50.18%); electrical machinery (51.98%); ships (66.81%); furniture and other wood products (54.01%); and fish (67.21%).

Steel mill
The Basque steel industry accounted for 33% of total Spanish production and 100% of nonwelded tubes during the 1960s and 1970s.
Engraving from Johann George Heck: The Complete Encyclopedia of Illustration.

Imports, on the other hand, accounted for 30.6% of total resources, with 23.5% of goods purchased from Spain and 7% from other countries. Apart from the tremendous significance of steel and iron, the main imports were agriculture- and livestock-related, energy, basic and intermediate chemicals, industrial vehicles, foodstuffs, and textiles and clothing. Rates of all these products greatly exceeded the BAC's import average (in relation to total resources).

Table 5-2
Trade balance in Bizkaia, Gipuzkoa, and Araba (1972, billion pesetas)

Agriculture	−11.434
Raw materials and energy	−15.314
Capital and intermediate goods*	+57.532
Transportation material**	−0.833
Common consumption	−20.171
Transformation & final consumption chemicals	+15.656
Other sectors	+432
Total	+25.868

* Electrical appliances included.
** Automobiles Included.

Source: Caja Laboral Popular Yearbook.

Table 5-2 gives a compilation of the various balance-of-trade figures from 1972.

IMPORTS OF agriculture, raw materials, energy, and common consumer goods resulted in a net deficit of 46.919 billion pesetas in 1972—equivalent to 12% of total production. The combined effect of the net surplus of intermediate and capital goods companies (57.532 billion pesetas) on one hand and chemical production and final consumption (15.656 billion pesetas) on the other, however, resulted in a net surplus of 25.868 billion pesetas, or 6.6% of total production, with foreign markets.

SHORTAGE OF FACILITIES
The model of economic development discourages public spending in infrastructures, giving rise to large differences in the provision of social services among the terri-

Table 5-3
Evolution of the population of the Southern Basque Country (1960–81)

	Araba	Bizkaia	Gipuzkoa	Navarre
1960	133,742	751,014	473,951	406,838
1970	199,777	1,041,461	626,049	466,593
1981	257,850	1,189,278	694,681	509,002

Source: *Great Historical Atlas of the Basque World.*

tories. A report about greater Bilbao (including the outlying towns) indicates the necessity to devote more than 1,300 hectares to collective facilities (sociocultural, sports, educational, parks). Such an expanse would be equivalent to two-thirds of the land officially designated as industrial sites and nearly four times that devoted to facilities. It would require not only huge investments but also reorganization of the urban districts of an area with more than 900,000 inhabitants.

DEMOGRAPHIC EVOLUTION AND THE WORK MARKET
As Table 5-3 shows, the population increased, especially in Bizkaia, Gipuzkoa, and Araba. This increase includes both natural growth and the effects of the arrival of immigrants. The highest rate was that of Araba.

The evolution of the active population is shown in Table 5-4.

THE UNEMPLOYMENT rate increased from 0.46% in 1960 to 0.95% in 1971. The unemployment rate in 1975 was 0.6% in Araba, 3.32% in Gipuzkoa, 6.7% in Navarre, and 3.54% in Bizkaia. Three years later, unemployment ranged from 14.2% to 16.5% in all the territories except for Araba.

The distribution of the active population by sector between 1955 and 1975 shows that, after twenty years, agricultural employment fell from 24.5% to 10.8% of the total active population.

As late as 1975, 20.9% of Navarre's active population was employed in the primary sector. In the industrial sector, the largest relative increases occurred in the recently industrialized Araba and Navarre. The percentage of the active population employed in industry remained steady in Bizkaia (43%) and increased slightly in Gipuzkoa.

The Dynamics of the Working Class

In 1962, a general strike affected more than 50,000 workers. Significant wage increases were won despite the firings that resulted. From 1963 to 1966, a series of strikes erupted. Although illegal, they became a means of fighting for better wages. Labor conflicts were mainly over wage increases; improved working conditions (such as fewer working hours, lower retirement age, safety, and hygiene) were but secondary demands.

The growing importance of the Basque worker movement during the 1970s directly influenced wage gains,

Table 5-4
Active population (in thousands)

	Araba	Bizkaia	Gipuzkoa	Navarre
1960	58.4	344.9	210.4	176.2
1971	87	413	261.8	188
1975	91.6	438.9	274.3	184.1

Source: *Great Historical Atlas of the Basque World.*

although an economic crisis appeared during the second half of the decade.

Lesson five

BIBLIOGRAPHY
Fundación BBV. http://www.bbva.es.
University of Mondragón. http://www.muni.es.

LEARNING GOAL
Describe the main aspects of the Basque economic model from the 1970s until the beginning of the economic crisis.

WRITTEN LESSON FOR SUBMISSION
1. In what quantities were Basque goods exported? What relevance did some branches of Basque industry have within Spanish industry as a whole?
2. Was the evolution in demography and in the labor market similar in all the Basque territories?

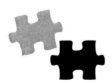

6 · Deindustrialization 1973–85

THIS CHAPTER covers a period of great crisis and restructuring of Basque industry. The basic sectors of Basque industry fell into depression in the Basque Autonomous Community (or BAC). The crisis did not have strong repercussions in the Foral Community of Navarre (or FCN), however, due to its late industrialization.[2]

In the BAC, 152,000 jobs were lost between 1975 and 1985, 73% of them in the industrial sector. This meant a 30% decrease in BAC industrial employment. The industrial crisis was less significant in Navarre, in which 17% of industrial jobs were lost over the same period.

First, this chapter characterizes the problems of the Basque industry, dividing these into three sections: the companies themselves, the industrial structure, and the general framework in which companies operate. The chapter then focuses on the weaknesses in public enterprise and foreign investment and finally reviews the process of restructuring in the 1980s.

PROBLEMS FOR COMPANIES

Basque manufacturers exhibit a significant lack of managerial and business culture. For example, the level of business cooperation is low and internationalization is scarce. Moreover, there are deficits in several aspects of business management, such as human resources, commercialization, and marketing.

SPECIALIZATION & STRUCTURE IN BASQUE INDUSTRY

Specialization is usually cited as one of the main causes of the crisis in Basque industry, especially in the case of the BAC. Concentration has been very high in sectors greatly affected by the crisis in international-level, basic, and mature sectors. BAC industry is relatively specialized in basic intermediate goods. The production of capital goods (equipment) is also important. However, the BAC is not a significant producer of consumer goods.

The most relevant sector of the BAC is metal products, which accounted for 21.1% of the industrial GAV (gross added value) in 1985. This sector includes a great variety of activities: foundry, forge, and impression; metal construction; and metal products. It is these last two in which the BAC is most highly specialized.

THE BASIC METAL sector, due to the importance of Basque siderurgy, has been dominant in the BAC for several decades. In 1972, it accounted for 24% of the total industrial GAV. Despite its crisis and the recession, the sector remained very important, accounting for 15.8% of the industrial GAV in 1985. In 1981, 32,225 workers were employed in siderurgy in the BAC, while the number declined to 12,183 in 1995.

The importance of nonelectric industrial machinery increased in the BAC during the crisis period. In 1972, it represented 5.1% of the industrial GAV; in 1985, 10.7%. Other sectors important to the BAC are vehicles and transportation material, electric material, and rubber.

In sum, although activity in some industrial sectors (such as nonelectric industrial machinery) increased during the period, the lack of creativity in the industrial and service sectors in the BAC is noteworthy. Hence the extreme recession experienced by these traditional Basque sectors.

The case of the FCN differs, as it specializes in the production of consumer goods (such as vehicles and the food sector). Although some Navarrese industrial sectors also receded during the crisis period immediately preceding the 1986 entrance into the European Eco-

Computers
New technologies (especially telecommunications) provide new possibilities for the expansion of economic activity.
Watercolor by Ingo Fast.

---

nomic Community, the key sectors performed well. Moreover, in contrast to the BAC, in Navarre, the loss of jobs in the industrial sector has been offset by an increase in service employment.

GENERAL FRAMEWORK OF COMPANIES
The general framework in which companies operate—the financial sector, labor market, economic policy, education system, services to firms, infrastructures, land

and environment, the climate and social values—has had a variety of weaknesses that decisively influenced the crisis.

With respect to the financial sector, the banking sector, not the stock market, is predominant in the Spanish state. Until 1975, the bank-industry relationship was of a bank closely interconnected with the country's industrial activity. In 1975, however, the banking industry began a radical policy of reducing investment in industry and lowering risks, reducing the credit-expired periods. State monetary policy was very restrictive between 1977 and 1992, exposing Basque industry to very high interest rates, indebtedness, and general financial worries.

PUBLIC ENTERPRISE AND FOREIGN INVESTMENT
Other factors contributing to the weakening of the Basque economy were lack of public companies and foreign investment.

Regarding public companies, they have been few and fundamentally controlled by the central state administration. In spite of the implantation of public companies in Spain since the 1940s, especially through the National Industry Institute (INI), public companies were largely insignificant in Basque industry until 1969. That year, in the shipbuilding sector, La Naval (Sestao) and Euskalduna merged with Cadiz Astilleros to create AESA.

OTHER EXAMPLES of Basque public companies controlled from Madrid include Petronor (Repsol), Babcock Wilcox (INI, nationalized in 1980), Altos Hornos de Vizcaya, and ACENOR (BCI during the restructuring of the 1980s). The process of restructuring undertaken by the central state administration of these companies, as noted later in this chapter, has had negative ramifications for the Basque economy.

Foreign investment was relevant in the Basque industry prior to the crisis. It was important in, among others, the food sector, tire sector (Michelin, Firestone, Bridgestone), transportation material, vehicles (Mercedes Benz), and electric equipment (General Electric Española, Westinghouse).

But, since the crisis, the BAC has not been attractive for foreign capital, in spite of the great efforts to this end. What little investment does exist is directed to revitalizing companies located in this community before the crisis. Navarre, in contrast, has been more successful, with the acquisition of the private SEAT by Volkswagen in the 1990s.

THE RESTRUCTURING PROCESS

In the face of this deep industrial crisis, some industrial restructuring, although belated, was undertaken in the 1980s by the central state administration and the Basque and Navarrese governments. In the case of the BAC, in 1981, two years after the signing of the Statute of Autonomy, Bizkaia and Gipuzkoa recovered the Concierto Economico with the state, which would regulate the fiscal and financial relations between the two administrations. Also in 1981, the regional development agency SPRI (Agency for Industrial Promotion and Restructuring), which was used to implement industrial policy, was created.

In Navarre, the Agency for the Development of Navarre (SODENA) was created in 1984 as an instrument to improve and generate new industrial projects under the direction of the government of Navarre. The policy developed in Navarre was not as involved as that in the BAC for several reasons, however: the crisis was less intense, and the jurisdictional powers assumed by the autonomous community were more limited.

The BAC (or Basque) government did not have full control over industry at the time because the central state administration retained a number of critical jurisdictions over both industry and labor.

The central administration retained jurisdiction over the restructuring of large companies, thus affecting sectors basic to the Basque economy, such as shipbuilding, siderurgy, and equipment. Private companies such as AHV, Acenor, Babcock Wilcox, Inespal, and AESA were no longer independent, instead coming under the central state administration's control.

Through a plan approved in 1985, called PRE (Economic Relaunching Plan), the Basque government was entrusted with the restructuring of fourteen other sectors, where small and midsize companies were predominant, such as machine tool, kitchen appliances, and paper factories. PRE lasted three years and disbursed 31.5 billion pesetas.

SPAIN'S 1986 incorporation into the European Economic Community (EEC) had some direct consequences for Basque industry. The sectors in the process of restructuring had to adapt to the community's norms. Transition periods were established in the internal market for the integration of certain sectors in order to provide time for restructuring. For example, in the siderurgy sector, the transition period lasted from 1986 to 1988.

The European Community, however, does not bear the responsibility for the restructuring undertaken by the central administration in those sectors under state control. In the siderurgy sector, for example, at the end of the transition period, the Spanish government left AHV and ACENOR on the verge of collapse. Nevertheless, Basque industry has been recovering since 1985. On one hand, the international economic situation has improved and, on the other, the effects of the anticrisis policies have been positive.

Lesson six

BIBLIOGRAPHY

Basque Government. Basque Country: a Social and Economic Guide. Gobierno Vasco.

———. http://www.euskadi.net.

Gómez Uranga, M., and G. Etxebarria. 2000. "Panorama of the Basque Country and Its Competence for Self-Government." *European Planning Studies* 8(4):521–535.

SPRI. The Investor Guide. SPRI.

LEARNING GOAL

Show the severe impact of the economic crisis of the mid-1970s on Basque industries.

WRITTEN LESSON FOR SUBMISSION
1. What factors provoked the severe crisis in Basque industry?
2. Was there a real process of industrial restructuring? What roles were played by the respective institutions?

7 · Economic indicators
Mid-1970s to mid-1980s

THE BASQUE economy has experienced business cycles of both great growth (such as the 1970s and late 1980s) and severe crisis in its evolution. One of the most severe crises took place from the mid-1970s to the mid-1980s.

In this sense, as observed in Table 7-1, the BAC enjoyed one of Spain's highest growth rates in the 1960s, allowing it to attain above-average levels of income per capita. The crisis had very adverse effects, reflected in the significant decrease experienced in per capita production. These and many other indicators are examined in the present chapter.

THE INTERNATIONAL ECONOMIC CRISIS
The international crisis created by the December 1973 Yom Kippur war reached Spain in 1975. It lasted a decade. The crisis had a severe impact on the Spanish economy, as it took place during a process of political

Table 7-1
GDP growth and GDP per capita in the BAC

		BAC	Spain
GDP annual	1960–75	8.1	7.1
growth rate (%)	1975–85	−0.3	1.8
GDP per capita	1960	37,014	22,073
(pesetas)	1975	216,813	159,691
	1985	807,358	725,430

Source: Banco Bilbao Vizcaya.

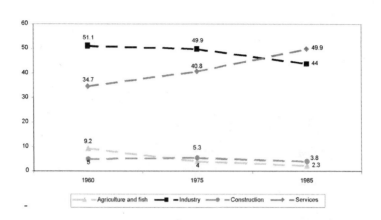

Figure 7-1. Evolution of the sectors in the BAC (%); services have grown as industry has decreased.

transition, in a country closely interdependent with the international (especially, European) economy and that did not have an adequate response.

THE ENERGY crisis of those years gave rise to a situation of stagflation, a combination of stagnation of production with inflation. As seen in Table 7-2, this situation greatly affected the development of the Basque economy in its convergence with the EEC countries.

The weight of some of the industrial sectors in crisis (siderurgy, shipbuilding, and equipment goods) in the industry's value added was higher in the BAC than in the EEC countries, causing their relative importance to decline. These negative factors clearly contributed to the BAC economy's lower industrial production and wealth levels with respect to the previous decade, as well as to the greater unemployment.

Table 7-2
Relative position of the BAC with respect to the average GDP per capita in the EEC (Average EEC = 100)

	1964	1975	1985
BAC	109.3	109.9	81.1
Total (Spain)	68.3	80.4	71.8

Source: Banco Bilbao Vizcaya.

THE IMPACT OF THE CRISIS ON THE INDUSTRIAL FRAMEWORK OF THE BAC

In the 1970s, the BAC's industry generated approximately 50% of total production, with more than 40% of the active population employed in this sector. As a result, the BAC was one of the main attraction poles for internal migration. On the other hand, the Basque economy's tertiarization was clearly inferior; this distinctive feature would have decisive consequences during the phase of economic crisis.

THE GREAT economic dependence on manufacturing production aggravated the mid-1970s energy crisis in the BAC, giving rise to a severe industrial crisis. The delay in the implementation of rationalization policies and diversification measures (which did not occur until the early 1980s) further increased the impact of the crisis.

As evident in Figure 7-1, industry's relative importance in the BAC's GDP decreased during the crisis years, with the role of services growing notably and noncyclically.

In contrast, both the agriculture and fishing sector and the construction sector declined significantly throughout the decade. The former continued its precrisis ten-

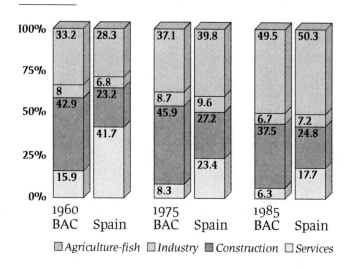

Figure 7-2. Evolution of employment by sector (%).

dency; the latter waned largely due to its cyclical nature and its sensitivity to the economy's oscillation.

REGARDING THE evolution of employment by sector, in 1960, the proportion of employment in the secondary sector was very high, above the average in Spain (where agricultural employment predominated). As shown in Figure 7-2, during the initial years of the crisis, employment in industry remained high, while that in the service sector increased and that in the agriculture and fishing sector decreased continuously. Finally, in the last years of crisis and industrial restructuring, employment in industry declined notably in comparison to the moderate decreases in the rest of Spain. In 1985, the tertiary sector became the major sector in the BAC economy (49.5% of the GDP) and accounted for the majority of employment.

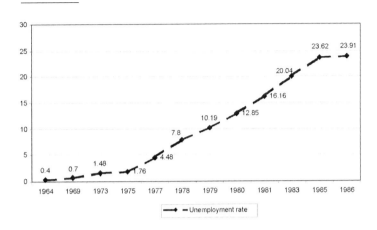

Figure 7-3. Evolution of the unemployment rate (%).

IT HAS TO BE remembered that during the 1950s and 1960s the BAC was a host region for migrants whose work further strengthened industrialization. The incorporation of women into the labor market was very limited, which explains the low unemployment rates (close to zero).

Beginning in 1975, as a result of the crisis, unemployment rates would increase, reaching the historical maximum of 23.91% in 1986. From that year until the early 1990s, they would decrease steadily.

CRISIS IMPACT IN PER CAPITA INCOME LEVELS

In sum, the deep crisis of the second half of the 1970s impacted strongly on the economy's per capita income levels, as shown in Table 7-4, which until the 1960s had been among the highest of Spain.

Thus, from clearly exceeding the national average per capita levels (in 1967, Spain's average income was 571,309 pesetas; that of Bizkaia, Gipuzkoa, and Araba

(National average = 100)

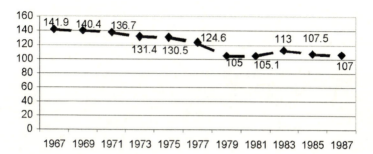

Figure 7-4. Evolution of per capita income of the BAC (%).

reached 810,795—70% greater); at the end of the crisis, it was only slightly higher (the Spanish average in 1985 was 903,374 pesetas, compared to the BAC's 971,531 pesetas).

Lesson seven

BIBLIOGRAPHY
Caja Laboral Popular. Yearbooks.
EUSTAT. http://www.eustat.es.
Fundación BBV. http://www.bbva.es.
INE. http://www.ine.es.
Jubeto, Y., Mariluz, S., and Zurbano, M. 2002. Euskal Herriko Ekonomia: Eraldaketa sozioekonomikoak Europako Batasuneko integrazio-prozesuan. Udako Euskal Unibertsitatea (UEU)

LEARNING GOAL
Describe the evolution of the Basque economy during the crisis using some economic indicators.

WRITTEN LESSON FOR SUBMISSION
How did the economic crisis of the 1970s influence the Basque industrial framework? In your answer, make use of the economic indicators.

8 · Development of Basque institutions

EVEN AFTER the regional institutions of the BAC and the FCN were established, the Spanish state retained important regulatory functions, sovereignty over many jurisdictions (including currency, the armed forces, general legislation, economic and welfare policies, and tax regulations), foreign trade relationships, and coordination in many areas. The combination of the demands based on a strong sense of Basque national identity and the historical legacy of foralism forced the state to acknowledge the distinctiveness of the Southern Basque Country. One result was the implementation of a separate tax system in the four Basque provinces. In the late 1970s, Spain began a process of transition to a democratic system of representation, more consistent with developed western countries. The state approved a Constitution that defined it in regional terms and established different ways for regions to achieve a degree of autonomy. As a result, the autonomous communities emerging from the Spanish Constitution received both administrative powers previously denied them and their own parliamentary assemblies. The state was not reconfigured as a federal system, however.

The Southern Basque territories recovered their own system of tax agreements with the state (called the Concierto Fiscal) before the actual Constitution was approved. This special system between the territories and the state had been abolished in its entirety by the goverment of General Franco in Gipuzkoa and Bizkaia. This idiosyncratic system had its roots in the loss of the Basque foral system in the nineteenth century; its recovery represented a singular exception in Spain.

Four-way cut
Foral Deputations distribute their money thus: state, BAC government, municipalities, and the rest for their own use.

THE EUROPEAN Union has been designing its regional map in recent years. The difficulty of governing in Keynesian terms and the existence of an increasingly competitive macroeconomic environment has necessarily shifted efforts towards policies that favor supply and local potential. Governing policies are therefore evolving toward training and encouragement of innovation at the most decentralized levels.

THE SPANISH CONSTITUTION FROM A SOCIOECONOMIC VIEWPOINT

From a socioeconomic viewpoint, the Spanish Constitution has a number of effects, among them:

1. The constitution establishes Spain's economic system along the lines of the principles of a developed capitalist state, thereby recognizing freedom of enterprise and ensuring principles of distributive justice and social welfare coverage.
2. It is a modern document (1978) that recognizes rights in line with a modern economy and society (such as environmental protection, workers' economic rights, training and recycling, consumer protection, economic modernization and development, and scientific development).
3. The state has absolute jurisdiction over all socioeconomic arenas that are traditionally controlled by a sovereign state, from the normal functioning of the currency and exchange of currencies to legislative and judicial regulations and general legal codes.
4. There is a Constitutional Jury that has the final say on jurisdictional issues among the different institutions. Most of the time, however, this body's interpretations do not seem to benefit the autonomous communities, such as the BAC and the FCN, since it has developed basic laws that overtly conflict with the jurisdictions exclusive to these communities.

THE BASQUE INSTITUTIONS FROM AN ECONOMIC POINT OF VIEW

The Foral Deputations are the Basque institutions that were originally in charge of collecting taxes. As a result, there have been a series of agreements with the government of the state (the Basque Quota and the Agreement in Navarre). Tax autonomy therefore preceded the constitution of the modern regional Spanish state that, through its Constitution, recognizes both the BAC and FCN as autonomous regions. Navarre's autonomy coincides with its own historical territory; the other three Basque provinces form a single autonomous region under a Statute of Autonomy inserted into the Spanish Constitution, with each of them keeping its own specific tax system.

As the Basque tax administrations collect the majority of taxes, it seems logical that a certain amount of money should be paid to the central government for funding activities out of their jurisdiction. The agreement that regulates this is called *cupo*, or "quota." The *cupo* is an amount determined by a commission formed by the Basque institutions and the central government every five years. This sum, to be paid to the central government by Basque institutions, is calculated on the basis of both those administrative powers that have been assumed and those that have not (Concierto Law May 1981; due for revision in December 2001 and finally revised in February 2002 and signed in March 2002 after long, hard discussions). How the Basque tax agreement with the state works is examined next.

The Basque tax administrations (Haciendas Forales) are entitled to insure, administer, pay, inspect, revise, and collect the taxes previously agreed upon in the Basque historical territories.

Some very real restrictions exist, however, due to the state's sovereignty over taxes previously agreed on (including part of the value-added tax) and because the tax system of the Basque territories must fulfill the following requirements: (1) Joint responsibility towards the rest of the regions of the state; (2) Coordination, tax harmonization; (3) Insertion in international treaties; (4) Effective pressure equivalent to that existing in the rest of the state; and (5) Respect of free circulation of capital and cooperation with state and local institutions.

The income of the Foral Deputations is distributed in the following way: one part is allocated for payment of the *cupo* to the state, another for the Basque government for its own finances, another for the municipalities in the territory, and the remainder is spent by the Deputation itself.

A brief look at the spending of the Foral Deputations reveals tax collection to be their most important function; also their most common allocations are those dealing with road infrastructure and social programs (welfare and poverty). As tax collectors, Deputations also work for other institutions (central goverment, Basque goverment, and municipalities).

DISTRIBUTION OF THE SHARE BETWEEN DEPUTATIONS AND THE BASQUE GOVERNMENT

The revenue collected by Deputations and shared with the Basque goverment has always been a source of conflict; the Deputation of each territory does not want to have a smaller budget, and each wants the Basque goverment to reinvest benefits into its territory in proportion to its contribution to the autonomous budget. The contribution of each territory to the general budget of the BAC also depends on annual tax collection.

TAXES ARE collected differently in each territory, and the process can therefore progress very rapidly in a territory one year and very slowly the next. In 1999, Bizkaia provided 51.76%, Gipuzkoa 32.60%, and Araba 15.64% of the Basque government's income. The balance between contribution and actual tax collection achieved during parliamentary mandate is established through an Interterritorial Compensation Fund to which

Home rule?
The regional institutions of the BAC and the FCN still yield to the Spanish state in important regulatory functions, on sovereignty over many jurisdictions, such as foreign trade relationships, and on coordination in many areas.
Illustration by Jens Bonnke.

---

both the Basque goverment and the three territories contribute.

SPENDING JURISDICTIONS OF THE BASQUE STATUTE OF AUTONOMY
The Basque Statute of Autonomy and El Amejoramiento del Fuero de Navarra promote the existence of parlia-

ments whose objective is both to approve the annual budget of goverments and to develop some laws and regulations concerning the current jurisdictions.

Among the spending jurisdictions of both autonomous communities, as elsewhere in Europe, those that stand out are the ones with the highest level of autonomy, especially education, health, and culture. A large segment of civil servants is employed in these fields in the Basque Country. Culture jurisdictions include Basque radio and television; industry is also attaining a high degree of importance in regional policies, and the Basque Country is somewhat idiosyncratic in this aspect. One jurisdiction exclusive to the Basque Country among all Spanish regions is its own, autonomous police force, which, given the historical Basque uniqueness, is viewed from within as an absolute necessity.

ONE ITEM related to economic matters appears in both the general budget of the Basque goverment and those of the Foral Deputations. In fact, the spending on infrastructure and public works by the three deputations in the BAC exceeds that of the Basque goverment. This can create conflict in the planning of roads, especially when the common interests of the BAC diverge from those of any or all of the three territories.

JURISDICTIONS ESTABLISHED BY EL AMEJORAMIENTO DEL FUERO DE NAVARRA

This autonomy agreement between representatives from the central state and some from Navarre, signed in 1982, resembles the BAC's statute with respect to economic jurisdictions. In the same manner that the payments of the tax administrations of the other territories are subject to the *cupo*, Navarre is subject to the *convenio*, or "agreement." The spending jurisdictions of the government of Navarre also focus on education and health; unlike the BAC, however, they do not cover radio and television, and Navarra's autonomous police force is not widespread. Moreover, despite the increasing importance of its industrial policy, when compared to the BAC, Navarre lacks experience in this domain, and its policies are quite simply less far-reaching. Navarre possesses an institution that controls public accounts corresponding to the BAC's Hacienda Foral but with an even longer tradition: the Cámara de Comptos (Chamber of Accounting).

AS THE ECONOMIC viability of an autonomous region as small as Navarre is doubtful, its incorporation into the BAC would allow it to benefit from well-integrated, large-scale economic systems. At present, for political reasons, the political party in government in Madrid openly opposes any cooperation between these two regional governments—even in cultural matters, and despite their ancient common roots, history, and language.

Lesson eight

BIBLIOGRAPHY

Gómez Uranga, M., and G. Etxebarria. 2000. "Panorama of the Basque Country and Its Competence for Self-Government." *European Planning Studies* 8(4):521–535.

Instituto Vasco de la Administración Pública. http://www.ivap.es.

Instituto Navarro de la Administración Pública. http://www.cfnavarra.es/INAP/index.HTML.

Lambarri, C., and A. Van Mourik, eds. 1998. *Tax Harmonization: The Case of the Economic Agreement between Spain and the Basque Country.* Fundación BBV.

Mata, J. M. 1998. "Nationalism and Political Parties in the Autonomous Community of the Basque Country: Strategies and Tensions." Working Papers, Institut de Ciencies Politiques i Socials, Barcelona.

LEARNING GOAL

Analyze the structure of institutions and jurisdictional powers of the territories of the Southern Basque Country (governments, administrations, *concierto, convenio*) in the framework of the Spanish Constitution.

WRITTEN LESSON FOR SUBMISSION
1. What do *concierto* and *convenio* mean?
2. How does the Basque government obtain its revenues?

9 · Basque economy and globalization

THE ECONOMY of the Southern Basque Country has changed from being encapsulated exclusively within the Spanish economy to increasingly projecting itself toward Europe and, to a lesser degree, non-European countries. This transition from autarky to greater integration into the international community has been connected to Spain's own opening up from the mid-1970s onwards, especially since its entry into the European Union in the mid-1980s.

The opening up process of the Basque economy accelerated during the 1990s as a result of the emergence of the European Economic and Monetary Union. The spread of economic globalization also contributes greatly to the increasing economic interaction between the Basque Country and the rest of the world. This greater integration of the Basque economy is reflected in its trade rates, which reveal that a greater percentage of Basque products goes abroad and that consumption of imported goods is increasing. While these indicators are neither absolute nor conclusive, they do demonstrate a clear tendency towards the integration of the Basque economy into the global milieu, with all the resulting consequences.

ECONOMIC GLOBALIZATION
The term *globalization* encapsulates the degree of internationalization of current economies. Without examining the term in detail, suffice it to say that *globalization* is the conjuncture of a multiplicity of international factors that coalesced during the 1990s, having consolidated over a historical process of economic internationalization.

Economic interaction among countries takes place in different fields and with an impact that varies with the times. International trade relationships are the most noticeable and oldest way of integration among differentiated economic circles. With the exception of the interwar period, international trade has grown noticeably thoughout the twentieth century. Due to progressive liberalization worldwide, more and more goods are traded in international markets.

Capital and financial resources are currently the best indicator of the freedom of movement in international markets. Beginning in the 1980s, states relinquished control over the entry and exit of capital. Since then, financial markets have been almost completely open. Mobility of capital between countries has therefore increased. This is known as financial globalization, and its most recent example is the consolidation of international securities markets.

FINANCIAL GLOBALIZATION also promotes a great degree of productive internationalization. Transnational companies face neither regulatory obstacles for capital entry nor repatriation of benefits of a country of destination. The strategies of big corporations lead to their establishing themselves in different economies so as to reap the specific benefits offered in each country. The consequence of these strategies is the growing integration of productive activity worldwide and an increase in productive specialization within countries.

THE BASQUE COUNTRY IN THE EUROPEAN UNION
While the Northern Basque Country has been part of the European Union since the treaty of Rome, the South entered the EU in 1986, as a result of membership being extended to Spain and Portugal. The EU is thus currently both the supranational framework of integration

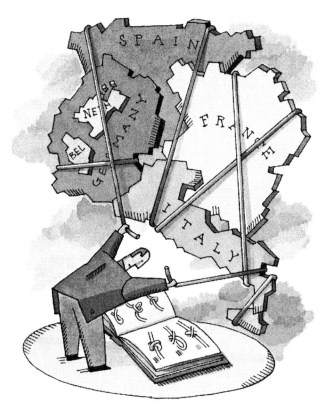

Europe
The EU has become the frame of reference within which basic economic regulation of the Basque economy is determined.
Watercolor by Robin Jareaux.

---

rently both the supranational framework of integration and the highest regulatory authority for the Basque economy. As will be shown, it is thus both the regional expression of the process of economic globalization and the international context for the Basque economy.

Since 1993, the European Union has formed a single market. Both goods and services and the factors affecting production—capital and work—therefore have total freedom of movement across borders within the EU. There is also a unified trade system (tariffs, quotas, and common trade restrictions) and a harmonization of the different policies of the member states (including security and foreign policy and policies dealing with the environment, industry, government jurisdictions, infrastructure, and agriculture). The unification of the main markets is, therefore, a tangible reality that is somewhat impeded by some factors associated with restrictions resulting from the EU's multicultural nature.

MOREOVER, MONETARY and economic convergence were to be realized in 2002 with the release of the euro as the single currency that replaces all others within its territory, including the peseta and the franc. The European System of Central Banks, formed by the Central Banks of the member states under the control of the European Central Bank, has the power to issue and regulate the euro. The European Central Bank is the institution that, at present, has jurisdiction over monetary policy matters throughout euro territory.

Consequently, the European Union has become the frame of reference within which basic economic regulation of the Basque economy is determined. With the exceptions of legal and socio-labor issues, the majority of economic policy is dictated from Brussels. Furthermore, the formation of a single European market leads to a reorientation of both economic flow and relationships of cooperation and competition between Basque economic agents towards policies increasingly dictated from beyond the Pyrenees.

THE EVOLUTION OF THE BASQUE FOREIGN SECTOR
The Basque foreign sector includes the full range of economic relationships between local and foreign economic

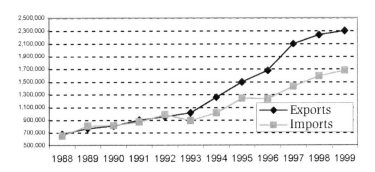

Figure 9-1. Evolution of the exports and imports of the Southern Basque Country (in millions of pesetas).

agents, both private and public. Trade relationships stand out, as do financial and productive relationships, generally associated with and following trade trends. In fact, commercial flow is the best barometer of the degree and structure of foreign insertion of a territory.

FOREIGN TRADE figures show that the Basque economy is becoming increasingly externally oriented. As seen in Figure 9-1, with the exception of those to the rest of the Spanish state, Basque exports tripled in nominal terms within a single decade (from 1988 to the present). In addition, the rise in imports into the Basque Country during the 1990s (240% in value) has been remarkable. The greatest rise in exports has taken place since 1993 for two reasons: the devaluation of the peseta twice that year (making exports less expensive and imports more expensive) and the start of a period of economic growth in the international and Basque economies (dynamizing imports and exports). In 1998 and, especially, 1999, however, the rhythm of foreign trade growth—both export and import—slowed.

This evolution of Basque imports and exports results in a trade surplus. As Figure 9-1 shows, until 1992 the value of imports and that of exports were very close, indicating a virtual trade balance; from 1993 onwards, however, especially in 1995, the trade surplus has increased (600 billion pesetas in 1999).

THE RAPID growth in Basque foreign trade during the 1990s is also reflected in the Basque economy's relatively high entry rates (exports/GDP) and penetration (imports/GDP). The entry rate of the economy of the Southern Basque Country in 1998 was around 30%, far above the entry rates of states like Spain (18%), France (22%), and Germany (23%), and very close to those of Austria, Denmark, Finland, and the average of the European Union-15. Although the penetration rate is lower

Table 9-1
Distribution of exports according to sector, 1998 (%)

FCN	Imports	Exports	BAC	Imports	Exports
Energy	0.60	–	Energy	11.70	3.90
Agriculture	11.50	7.00	Agriculture	9.28	3.70
Chemicals	8.20	5.15	Chemicals	4.56	2.62
Textiles, footwear	1.50	1.00	Plastics, rubber	6.83	8.19
Paper	2.28	4.54	Paper	3.80	2.67
Metal products	9.91	5.10	Metal products	25.13	22.17
Capital goods	29.03	17.70	Capital goods	28.94	49.66
Transportation material	35.64	56.00	Other manufactured goods	9.51	6.44
Others	1.34	3.51	Others	0.25	0.65
Total	100	100	Total	100	100

Source: EUSTAT and the government of Navarre.

(approximately 22%), it, too, is situated around the European Union median. Thus, leaving aside trade with the rest of the state, as a result of the dynamic situation of the 1990s, the Basque economy can be considered rather open to foreign trade.

The distribution of exports and imports by sector shown in Table 9-1 defines the relative importance of different activities in the opening up process. With regard to exports, capital goods is the most important sector in the Basque economy, increasing to account for nearly half of BAC exports in 1998 and a significant percentage of Navarre's exports (18%) that same year.

METAL PRODUCTS is another sector that strongly (albeit decreasingly) contributes to the dynamism of exports. This is especially so in the BAC, where they account for just under one-fourth of all exports. The automobile industry has been responsible for more than half the export output of Navarre, despite the fact that it declined by 6% throughout the 1990s. Concerning imports, the three types of goods already mentioned, as well as agriculture and energy, combine to account for the sharp increase in the volume of Basque imports.

COMMERCIAL INSERTION OF THE BASQUE ECONOMY
After noting the Basque economy's outward dynamism and increasing expansion to foreign markets, it is important to indicate how this increasing economic integration is taking place mainly within the European Union.

To start with, although the Spanish market is still very important for Basque goods, it is losing ground as the primary destination. While the sale of goods to the rest of the state accounted for 60% of the BAC's GDP in 1985 (prior to Spain's entry into the EU), ten years later the amount declined to 36%. During the same period, BAC

Freedom of capital movements
Beginning in the 1980s, states relinquished control over the entry and exit of capital.
Illustration by Jens Bonnke.

---

exports to the EU (excluding Spain) doubled in relative terms (10% of the BAC's GDP in 1985 compared to 19.6% in 1995).

B ASQUE TRADE thus increasingly looks to Europe. One example is that BAC exports to the EU (excluding Spain) increased from 60% of the total export output in 1993 to 70% in 1999. The preferred EU destinations are France (27% of the BAC total to the EU), Germany (24%), Italy (12%), and the United Kingdom (10%). Navarrese exports to the EU decreased slightly during the 1990s, representing 83% of the total output in 1999. The most important destinations within the EU are France (27%), Germany (24%), the United Kingdom (14%), and Italy (11%). Navarre's trade with the EU was also very intense during the 1980s because networks were encouraged by the large amount of European capital in the foral community.

Regarding imports, their EU origin is even more significant. Nearly three quarters of imports into the BAC and 83% of imports into Navarre came from the EU in 1999. In fact, the four countries previously mentioned are the leading importers—notably France and, especially, Germany—due to Navarrese production's heavy dependence on imports from the latter.

In short, the economic interaction seen in the trade ties between the Basque Country and the European Union is very high, and it has been rising throughout the 1990s. This process of growing integration into the larger European economy will be reinforced with the economic union and the circulation of the euro in the coming years. The Basque economy's position within the global economic environment can be seen in its increasing involvement in the regional division of labor within European production. Thus, as a result of full economic interaction, the productive structure of the Basque Country is gradually becoming more integrated within an economically coherent European Union.

Lesson nine

BIBLIOGRAPHY

Camara de Comercio de Araba. http://www.camaradealava.com/.

Camara de Comercio de Gipuzkoa. http://www.cscamaras.es/camaragipuzkoa/camaragipuzkoa.html.

Camara de Comercio de Navarra. www.camaranavarra.com

Caja Laboral Popular. Several yearbooks.

LEARNING GOALS

1. Identify the level of economic integration of the Basque Country in the rest of the world, especially the European Union.
2. Show the impact of economic globalization during the 1990s on the economy of the Basque Country.
3. Document the evolution of the Basque foreign sector during the past decade.

WRITTEN LESSON FOR SUBMISSION

1. Compare the foreign sectors of Basque international commerce with the total sectorial production. Is there a correlation between the two?
2. What are the similarities and differences between the main imports and exports of the BAC and FCN? What are the reasons for these?

10 · Jurisdiction
Basque territories within the European Union

THE EVOLUTION OF THE NATION-STATE
Until the end of the Keynesian period (also known as the welfare period), the most developed nation-states maintained a certain capacity to regulate the economy inside their own borders. They controlled monetary movement within their national territory and capital inflow and outflow.

IN SUCH A context, the state carried out economic policies of a "national" nature, which meant, among other things, determining the interest rate and attempting to control the exchange rate.

After the crisis of the 1970s, the reorganization of world capitalism resulted in an increased internationalization of capital flow. In this context, mainly in the geostrategic framework of the European Union, states lost their capacity to establish their own monetary or exchange policies. Consequently, growth and, especially, employment targets are a thing of the past. The policy coordination among European Union states necessary for the creation of the single currency serves as a structural hindrance to macroeconomic adjustments by each state. It especially affects the populations of the weaker states, such as Spain. The "necessary control of inflation" demands of the states strict labor and socioeconomic discipline, among the most important jurisdictions left to the states.

The task of the French and Spanish governments in this phase of internationalization of capital consists of realigning the levels of sovereignty they maintain and sometimes reinforce. The "jurisdictional boundaries" are not stable but move depending on compromises determined by EU membership.

European nation-states are becoming more and more corporatist. Increasingly, they share jurisdiction with other states. They reinforce their authority in other fields and establish a share with other territories within them. Each state, nevertheless, continues to exercise the authority of its sovereignty. One of the areas in which nation-states still find their greatest degree of legitimacy within the EU framework is as the characteristic "welfare state"—mainly in the control of social security and employment laws. The welfare state thus "helps increase national identity and unity" (Keating and Loughlin, 1996). Jurisdiction in social affairs is both a symbol and an instrument of solidarity and national cohesion. It is perhaps thus understandable why the transfer of social security from the Spanish state to the Basque Autonomous Community is such a sensitive matter.

THE QUESTION OF JURISDICTION

The concept of *jurisdiction* (*competencia*) is associated with control over the political, legislative, normative, and judicial bodies; this is what is conventionally understood as the state.

IT IS RESTRICTIVE to link sovereignty with the state. Social and economic life are more varied and have aspects not directly connected with the scope of the state—for example, a whole network of informal relationships and some aspects of management, especially in transnational companies.

However, all the habitual references to the concepts of *jurisdiction* and *sovereignty* are circumscribed by the dominion of the state—or, more precisely, that of public matters, including the European Union and international organizations—and its regulatory role.

Greater jurisdiction of the different "territories" does not function as an à la carte menu to which each

Difference of opinion
Jurisdiction seldom allows regions and nations to do as they please. They progress by pressures and arguments, opinions and strategies.
Engraving from Jim Harter: Men, A Pictorial Archive.

"region" or "nation" gains access as it pleases. The process is dialectical and is characterized by pressures, arguments, strategies, opinions, powers, and so on. The states have implicitly imposed certain jurisdictional limitations.

BRIEFLY ANALYZING the power still to be transferred from the central state to the Basque Autonomous Community, the areas of employment and social security are by far the most relevant, but also the most difficult to transfer. This is so, first of all, because they would include elements that generate high revenue (unemployment subsidies and social security). Such programs are supported by extensive legislative and normative bases, which belong to those jurisdiction areas zealously preserved by the EU states.

A VARIETY OF the jurisdictions included in the BAC's Statute of Autonomy remain untransferred. Some deal with financing investment projects (highways); others would regulate markets (bank and credit, insurance, stock market, and hydrocarbon); and, lastly, others would enable a greater autonomy in public policy (the public sector of the state, research, official credit, harbors, and airports).

JURISDICTION IN THE TOP-LEVEL REGIONS

As has been pointed out, all stateless nations or regions at the highest jurisdictional level within developed countries currently have very similar limitations. This is not a matter of chance. The evolution of the European Union follows a paradigmatic model in which limits to sovereignty are defined by structural elements and tendencies such as:

1. The necessity to determine the space for both capital movement and the development of wider-range markets throughout the EU. This leads to the process now culminating in the euro and in the liberalization of strategic sectors. Moreover, it results in (a) oligopolistic European concentrations rather than national monopolies, and (b) European central monetary policies rather than national monetary and macroeconomic exchange policies. In other words, the boundaries of state operation are fundamentally different. In losing the jurisdiction, states are reduced to mere managers in the most "macro" areas. Besides, new jurisdictions are established, or at least shared, thereby circumscribing real state sovereignty to those

areas—including social, employment, culture, and everyday life—through which greater legitimacy can be gained.
2. The reluctance on the part of richer countries to share wealth. It is understandable that the middle and working classes in those countries do not want to be disadvantaged or see their production levels and their social advantages diminished.
3. The difficulty or impossibility to achieve more common policies stems mainly from several factors: cultural, linguistic, and historical differences, which prevent the formation of a more legitimized political government.

The result is that the states can and do maintain their reason for being, mainly in the following areas:
a. Everything involving redistribution within their borders, from the tax system to social security and other services.
b. Everything related to internal configuration and workforce rights.
c. International representation of all the territories within the boundaries of their sovereignty.
d. 1. Basic regulations concerning the organization of economy and society, although some of them may be coordinated by or simply subordinated to international authorities.
2. The creation and use of general infrastructures.
e. The preservation of internal order and the status quo, internationally awarded.
f. The organization of public spaces related to culture, communication, and education.
g. Policies regarding industry, technology, the primary sector, and certain services.
h. Others.

From the point of view of the more local jurisdictions of top-level stateless nations or regions, they could obtain jurisdictions of type f and occasionally some of types d and a, especially regarding tax matters. Three scenarios could be considered:
1. Top-level nations or regions generally, and others occasionally, may have jurisdiction over most management matters.
2. States allow no participation whatsoever.
3. States allow at least the top-level nations or regions the maximum permitted by the international context.

The integration of the Spanish state into the then-EEC, and more specifically the enforcement of the Treaty of Maastricht, means a substantial change in state sovereignty. The constitution is ceding sovereignty, and in this process it is not strictly necessary for the nominal jurisdiction held by the state simply to disappear; it is sufficient if, without disappearing, the jurisdiction is emptied of content.

IN THIS RESPECT, for example, among the thirty-two areas the Spanish Constitution recognizes as exclusively under state jurisdiction (article 149), the following typology could be suggested:
1. Ten out of the thirty-two are retained by the state with complete autonomy. These include only two out of the seven directly belonging to the socioeconomic sphere: (a) labor legislation, and (b) basic legislation and the social security system.
2. Twelve jurisdiction areas are directly linked to policies or to more general decisions of the European Union.
3. Five jurisdiction areas are subject to decisions of the EU.

4. Five jurisdiction areas imply mere management or execution of the European guidelines.

Consequently, an estimate—more qualitative than quantitative—could be made of the degree of the Spanish state's loss of sovereignty in this exclusive jurisdiction during the last phase of incorporation into the European Union and the creation of a single currency.

With regard to jurisdictions under exclusive control of the state, approximately 30% of the content has been shown to have been ceded. Had it been more intensely analyzed, the result might have shown an even greater loss of sovereignty.

The leading policy makers of the Spanish government observe the gradual deterioration of the state's jurisdictional framework during its integration in the EU with preoccupation.

THE EVOLUTION towards the single currency does not provide the most conducive environment for the development or maintenance of a jurisdictional framework like the one held by the territories of the Southern Basque Country. In fact, tax homogenization in the European Union, in accordance with free movement of capital, will affect Basque jurisdictional control over corporate taxes, income tax, and inheritance transfer. The tendency towards the improvement of private financial conditions at the expense of public ones does not provide optimal conditions for the consolidation of sovereignty, which would require reinforcement of the public sector. In addition, the previously mentioned process of European unification provokes inflexibility, as it would eliminate certain resources that could temporarily encourage anticyclical policies for fighting unemployment. Lastly, the European project, which grants exclusive representa-

Table 10-1.
Exclusive state jurisdiction versus top-level region jurisdiction.

Jurisdictional scope
Achievable by top-level regions

In Basic Regulations	**In Management**
a, certain parts of the financial sector.	c, case (Flemish, Scottish, and some Lander)
Specific case of agreements d-1 and d-2.	a, partial
Coordination (subordinate) with state planning.	b, partial
	d, partial (some cases CAV)1
f, but coordinated with the state.	e, partial
g.	f, may be exclusive or coordinated.
	g and h.

In Basic Regulations	**In Management**
From a to e.	Part of a.
Part of f.	Part of b and e.
Part of g.	Part of c.
Part of h.	Part of d.
	Part of f.
	Part of g.
	Part of h.

tion in the European government (The Council of Europe) to its member states, is clearly disadvantageous for the interests of many regions.

Lesson ten

BIBLIOGRAPHY

Bachtler, J., and I. Turok. 1997. *The Coherence of EU Regional Policy.* London: Regional Studies Association.

Gómez Uranga, M., and G. Etxebarria. 2000. "Panorama of the Basque Country and Its Competence for Self-Government." *European Planning Studies* 8(4):521–535.

Keating, M., and J. Loughlin. 1996. *The Political Economy of Regionalisms.* London: Frank Cass.

Tickell, A., J. Peck, and D. Peter. 1997. "The Fragmented Region: Business, the State and Economic Development in Northwest England." In *Regions and the New Europe*, M. Rhodes, ed., European Policy Research Unit Series.

LEARNING GOAL

Describe the economic jurisdiction of the territories of the Southern Basque Country within the framework of the European Union and the Spanish Constitution.

WRITTEN LESSON FOR SUBMISSION

1. Do all substate regions in the European Union have the same economic jurisdictions as developed nation-states?
2. Which jurisdictions are under exclusive control of the Spanish state? Which jurisdictions are shared between the state on one hand and the BAC and FCN on the other?

11 · **Service industry**
in the Southern Basque Country

DISTRIBUTION OF the main sectors of economic activity is known to be the outcome of complex economic processes with similar historical developments in western countries. The importance of the Southern Basque Country's three economic sectors, measured against their contributions to employment and production, is therefore not very different from neighboring economies.

Service activities play an essential role in the majority of western countries, while agriculture tends to be marginal. As shown in Figures 11-1 and 11-2, this is also true for the Basque economy, as determined by the contribution of each sector to employment and generated gross added value (GAV). The figures indicate how the service industry contributes 54% to production and 58% to the rate of full employment in the Southern Basque Country.

Development of the respective sectors varies by territory. The processes of decrease in agricultural activities, industrial decline or activity, and the increasing importance of services affect the four historical territories differently in both time and degree. The result is reflected in the varied composition of the sectors in each territory. The data supplied by the INE (National Institute of Employment) portrays this on the basis of the contribution of each sector to the figure of full employment in the territory. The marked presence of the service industry in the Bizkaian economy (62.9% of full-time workers) underscores not only the progress of services induced by the concentration of population in towns, but also the great impact of industrial decline. The relative lack of significance of the primary sector and a mere

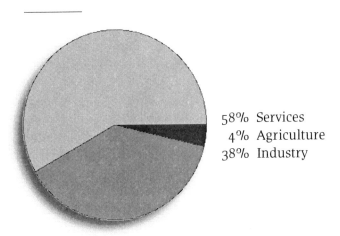

Figure 11-1. Distribution of the workforce by sector in the Southern Basque Country.

- 58% Services
- 4% Agriculture
- 38% Industry

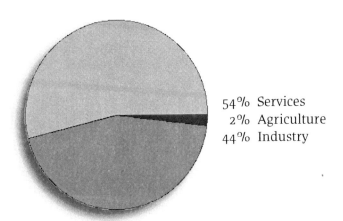

Figure 11-2. Distribution of gross added value (market prices) in the Southern Basque Country.

- 54% Services
- 2% Agriculture
- 44% Industry

36% of industrial employment (ranking Bizkaia behind the other territories) complete the sectorial panorama.

ARABA AND GIPUZKOA are also more active in service than in the other sectors: 55% and 56%, respectively. In both territories, industry is still relatively very important in comparison to the 25% to 35% of full employment in other western countries. The increase of services thus accompanies a growing industrial framework. Navarre's is also basically a service economy, although to a lesser extent than the other territories. The industrial sector is also significant, while the agriculture sector is of much greater importance than in the other territories of the Southern Basque Country.

GENERAL TENDENCIES OF SERVICES

Figures 11-1 and 11-2 confirm the supremacy of service activity in the economy of the Southern Basque Country, both overall and within each territory. Mirroring the trajectory of production in other European countries, the Basque Country has undergone processes of reorganization within the different sectors throughout the second half of the twentieth century. The result is service dominance throughout the Basque productive sector, as seen in Figure 11-3.

Service dominance, however, is a recent phenomenon in the Basque Country. Just twenty years ago, this sector did not even account for 40% of full-time workers. After the initial impact of the industrial crisis in 1985, service employment was predominant only in Bizkaia. It was not until the 1990s that services would become the leading sector within the structure of the Basque economy as a whole.

This belated process of service dominance results from a structural change that affects each historical territory differently. Such change occurred in the Bizkaian

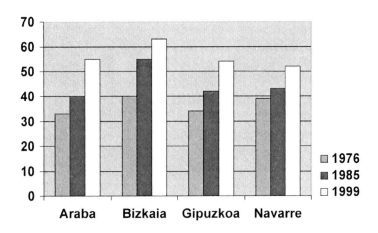

Figure 11-3. Distribution of employment in the service sector, by territory.

economy at the same time as the rapid collapse of industry during the past two decades. This collapse has contributed both directly and indirectly to the significant relative sectorial growth of services in Bizkaia, although it is not the only factor.

THE INCREASING importance of services in Navarre and Araba is not an obstacle for industry, which, despite its later start, continues to progress. Services and industry are currently experiencing parallel development in these two territories.

This chapter does not include a thorough analysis of the rise to dominance of the service sector in the Basque economy, which in great part parallels trends in other western economies. In explaining the progress of the service sector, however, the importance of its interconnection with the significant industrial framework in Basque production is impossible to ignore. Other factors also merit mention: new consumer habits that encourage a final demand of services, a rise in purchasing power during the past two decades, and the development of institutions as public service administrators.

The development of services in the Basque Country is clearly both slow and behind the times, due to poor capitalization and other factors that include a steep industrial decline that hinders the potential boost of services to businesses, an increasing presence of foreign capital, and the sheltering nature of services for fired industrial employees.

Table 11-1
Distribution of the gross added value (market prices) of services in the Southern Basque Country (%)

	1980 BAC	1980 FCN	1995 BAC	1995 FCN
Trade, restoration, and repairs	27.5	31.4	23.2	20.5
Catering industry	6.5	5.8	7.5	8.1
Transportation and annexes	11.8	7.1	9.0	7.8
Communications	3.4	2.9	3.6	4.5
Credit and Insurance	0.2	-0.5	3.7	0.3
Estate rental	20.2	22.3	16.4	19.6
Other services	11.3	7.7	13.7	14.0
Education	4.1	5.2	6.3	7.1
Health	5.6	7.8	6.9	10.2
Public administration	9.4	10.2	9.5	7.8
Total services	100.0	100.0	100.0	100.0

Source: Input-output tables of the BAC and FCN.

ACTIVITIES OF THE SERVICE INDUSTRY: COMPOSITION AND EVOLUTION

The service sector includes various activities, and diversity is its main characteristic. Services range from those provided to private persons to those provided to public or commercial businesses. But services also differ in their technological content and level of productive sophistication: cleaning services do not have much in common with engineering or telecommunication companies. It is therefore essential to itemize the different spheres of service activities.

THE FIGURES IN Table 11-1 are useful in that they reflect the internal productive structure of service activities for 1980 and 1995 in both the BAC and the FCN. Recently, trade, restoration, and repairs have predominated in the Southern Basque Country (23.2% of the total gross added value of services in the BAC and 20.5% in the FCN). Estate rental (16.4% and 19.6%, respectively) and other commercial and personal services (13.7% and 14%, respectively) follow closely. However, with regard to their dynamism, there is a significant difference between trade and estate rental on one hand and other services on the other. This last category has taken on an increasingly significant role within the sector since 1980 due to the great upswing in services to businesses, while the former lost ground throughout the 1980s and early 1990s. Transportation and annexes have also lost importance in the total GAV of services, although this decline affects only the southern part of the Basque Country.

In public administration, the evolution is one of general decline, since its contribution to gross added value in the service sector in the BAC has remained around 9.5%, while in the FCN it diminished sharply from 10.2% in 1980 to 7.8% in 1995.

The education and health sectors, in contrast, gained in relative importance in all territories during those fifteen years. Catering is a rapidly growing industry, increasing in relative importance due to the recent growth of tourism. Lastly, the communications sector is also expanding quickly as a result of its recent deregulation and the impact of new information technologies.

IN SUMMARY, the pattern of services in the economy of the Southern Basque Country is very similar to that in neighboring European countries: an expansion of the services that are the most capital intensive and generate higher added value (services to businesses, communications, education) and a greater dynamism of public services and catering, which are intertwined with recent aspects of local economic development.

Lesson eleven

BIBLIOGRAPHY
Bilbao Metropoli 30. http://www.bm30.es.
EUSTAT. http://www.eustat.es.
Government of Navarre. http://www.cfnavarra.es.

LEARNING GOAL
Describe the importance of the service sector to the Basque economy.

WRITTEN LESSON FOR SUBMISSION
1. What is the public share of the service activities in the BAC?
2. What are the general tendencies of services in the BAC?

12 · Infrastructures
Factors of regional development

THE POTENTIAL for internal economic development within a region depends on cultural and political variables, such as the training of its business class, ethics of work, cooperation between employers and unions, educational system, and qualification of its workforce.

To understand regional development completely, however, it is necessary to take the systems that carry information, goods, and people into account. The creation of infrastructure networks—physical networks (investment in physical capital in economic terms)—builds internal cohesion within a region and establishes essential outward links with other regions and spaces.

The creation of infrastructural networks depends in great measure on political decisions, the risks that investors are willing to take, and the capacity of different economic, social, and political agents to reach agreements and make compromises.

A poor infrastructural network hinders a region's internal development. There is a direct relationship between a region's endogenous growth and the network that connects to other regions within the state. Only with capacity for internal development can outward infrastructures grow and improve. A strong internal network always attracts investment for infrastructural projects with external links. The absence of development in one area leads investment away, to more favorable locations.

In traditional economic theory, infrastructures are known to have a direct influence on a region's productive activities. Infrastructural improvement increases the productivity of investment by reducing private costs, thereby generating an increase in both GDP per capita and the employment rate within the region. Infrastructures combine with other factors, such as private capital stocks and workforce, to determine the growth of regional GDP.

An existing infrastructural network is a clear incentive for businesses when they decide where to invest. And yet, infrastructures in themselves do not boost development but rather coevolve with it.

Factors such as location, clustering, and the structure of production have a direct influence on a region's development. Infrastructural networks in themselves do not promote regional development; they are a necessary, but insufficient, condition for the economic growth of a region.

INFRASTRUCTURAL NETWORKS IN EUROPE
European infrastructures have thus far been limited to state territories. Markets, technical capabilities, and legal and standardization problems have been the product of laws and regulations valid exclusively within states themselves. This frame of reference, however, is undergoing significant changes. The emergence of a common market (and in 1993 a single market) and the development of a European legislative framework have given rise to a group of European networks.

THE INTERNATIONALIZATION of capital makes it necessary to transcend the concept of state networks. The circulation of information, transport of energy, and highways and railways are all European. All obstacles to their development should therefore be removed. The process would start with the regulation and organization of the networks by the public sector and would emphasize the homogenization and harmonization of regula-

Bypassed
The building of trans-European connections sometimes further increases interregional differences of accessibility and economic opportunity throughout the European Union.
Watercolor by Robin Jareaux. Photograph from PhotoDisc, Inc.

tions, technical terms, and so on. The harmonization of the distinct infrastructural networks is considered one of the EU's greatest challenges.

TRANS-EUROPEAN networks emerge and grow more as a connection among centers of some relevance than as a continuum in a well-balanced supranational organization. Networks linking metropolitan areas are promoted. Some regions are thus merely crossed by infrastructural networks that connect centers belonging to other regions.

New transportation infrastructures tend to be built within and among central regions because of their greater transportation demand. Consequently, as long as capacity grows more quickly than demand, trans-European networks will mostly benefit Europe's dominant regions.

FURTHERMORE, THE building of trans-European connections sometimes further increases interregional differences of accessibility and economic opportunity throughout the European Union. Provision of roads and railways varies greatly between the richer regions of the center and the poorer regions on the periphery. The impact of the improvement of transportation is difficult to empirically verify. Attempts to explain the changes to economic indicators (of economic growth, for example) in terms of infrastructural investment have failed. The improvement of infrastructural networks has important effects on regional development only when the bottleneck effect is properly dealt with and eliminated.

INFRASTRUCTURAL NETWORK FINANCING AND MACROECONOMIC RESTRICTIONS

A series of restrictions making the different public administrations fulfill their requirements in matters including public deficit, public debt, and inflation are currently imposed and accepted in the European Union. The stability agreements reached by the governments of the EU lead to significant restrictions in public expenditure, with the most severe being in social programs. But they are also decisive in the ability to finance, operate, and maintain infrastructural projects that are usually very expensive. This explains private sector participation in financing these projects. Such participation is rewarded with exploitation rights for extended periods. This practice does not correspond with the interests of society as a whole. It is often the solution to purely economic and financing needs and the consequence of the neoliberal policies adopted by all public administrations. Such policies, however, largely limit capacity for management and social redistribution.

The financial requirements are so great that it becomes necessary to obtain funds from all the institutions. Regional governments thus endanger other activities because they believe that regional infrastructural improvement will bring more investment.

THE MAIN jurisdictional problem for the regions is that, in order to promote infrastructural policies, they have to establish priorities before going into heavy debt; otherwise, they would endanger other allocations. On the local level, such options and priorities can become irreversible. It seems important, therefore, to encourage agreements by better informing citizens about the various projects and alternatives and even organizing referenda for the consideration of projects of special interest.

THE ROLE OF THE EU, STATES, AND REGIONS IN INFRASTRUCTURAL POLICIES

The policy of transportation infrastructure in the European Union is contained in a report known as "The White Book about Employment," written by the then-president of the European Comission, Jacques Delors. This report includes all the most pressing economic problems of the member states. It argues that the most critical of these, unemployment, would be solved with greater, more sustained economic growth. Larger, better transportation and telecommunications networks would enable the exchange of goods, people, and information at great speed and over long distances, thereby ameliorating the problem.

The European Union considers the support of plans and initiatives of the member states among its objectives, as long as such projects are considered in the interest of Europe. The "community stamp" seeks to serve as a guarantee for movable private capital by offering financial support and loan guarantees to reduce administrative-financial risks.

The structure of an integrated market demands coordination and the creation of directives over infrastructural links of European design. But this point is subject to two major restrictions: (1) the necessity to respect the macroeconomic orientations related to deficit and accepted levels of public debt, and the regulations imposed by the policies of the community jurisdiction; and (2) the need to promote the development of less advanced regions in the EU through crucial infrastructural projects.

THE REASON BEHIND the Directive Plan of Infrastructure (PDI), designed in 1993 by the Spanish government, lies in the EU's transportation and infrastructural policies, to which all state and regional infrastructures in view must conform. This plan thus has the integration of the Iberian peninsula into the network of European infrastructures among its objectives. Different departments and levels of administration (the state, the autonomous community) can therefore benefit by financing these projects with the various structural and cohesion funds from the European Union. Because state governments are in charge of negotiating and administering such funds, however, and they usually distribute them by political criteria, conflicts between states and regions are common.

This situation is marked by competition among territories for more funding for their infrastructural projects, thus instigating confrontation and rivalry among the autonomous communities. Each claims highways, high-speed trains, ports, and other such projects for itself.

Transportation infrastructures have become the star projects of the new regional policies, in both more economically dynamic regions and those in decline. In both cases, the dominant institutional discourse converts them into a lifeline and hope for regional revitalization.

CONCLUSION

This chapter demonstrates the importance of the European institutional framework and member states to the formation of infrastructural policies and, more specifically, in the design and funding of networks. In fact, this institutional framework limits and conditions the potential for regional protagonism in infrastructural policy formation.

LACK OF A specifically regional infrastructural policy conditions the potential for both internal territorial coherence and connection with other territories. Furthermore, the social distribution of the influence of these infrastructures is conditioned in a way that usually serves to widen already existing social and spatial disparities.

The more balanced, coherent, and homogenous development of a region does not arise from the large infrastructural networks in existence. The expansion and fortification of infrastructures within one country would require the development of interregional networks. The internationalization of large infrastructural networks is no guarantee of a more integrated regional development. On the contrary, it promotes already consolidated centers. In this context, it is difficult to imagine that

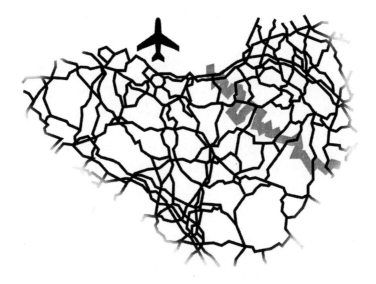

Transport network
If communication infrastructure is to provide greater cohesion within the Basque Country, it should reinforce internal connections and relationships.

---

connections among intraregional centers, such as Bilbao-Pamplona-San Sebastian, would be promoted as a result of the expansion of European networks. Greater cohesion would require more balance in the development of the different parts of the Basque Country and promotion of infrastructural networks that not only allow good connections with distant centers and regions but also reinforce internal connections and relationships at all levels.

Lesson twelve

BIBLIOGRAPHY
Biehl, D. 1991. "The Role of Infrastructure in Regional Development." In *Infrastructure and Regional Development*, R. Vickerman, ed. London: Pion Limited.
CEC, DG III. 1990. Trans-European Networks.
CEC. 1991. Transport in a Fast-Changing Europe. Group Transport 2000.
Gómez Uranga, M., and G. Etxebarria. 1994. "Institutional Agreements and Long-term Infrastructure Finance Schemes." Challenges to Institutional and Evolutionary Economic Theory: Growth, Uncertainty and Change. EAEPE 1994 Conference, October 27–29. Copenhagen, Denmark.

LEARNING GOALS
1. Introduce infrastructural networks as fundamental elements of regional development.
2. Provide a vision of infrastructural policies in Europe.

WRITTEN LESSON FOR SUBMISSION
1. Do infrastructural networks promote economic development?
2. What are the roles of the European Union, states, and regions in infrastructural financing and policies?

13 · Geography and infrastructure
The future

BRIEF HISTORICAL OVERVIEW

Throughout its history, the network of transportation infrastructures in the Basque Country has been configured by the necessities for connecting its districts and territories by trade and economic relationships with other countries and regions. In addition, a network of roads (built over the old roadways), rail networks, ports, and airports has surged, organizing and linking Basque territory. Villages and cities are therefore joined, and production centers connected with supplies and markets. People are also displaced—and, with them, information and culture in its broader sense.

The different means of transportation have developed in the existing transportation network. For example, when analyzing the road networks, the importance of ports in the Basque Country (both historical and current) and the introduction of the railway in the nineteenth century (with its impact upon the country's industrialization) cannot be ignored. The importance of airports, crucial connection points with other cities and countries that reach the four corners of the world, is also noteworthy.

IN EFFECT, the development and control of the main communication routes throughout the centuries have been linked to trade and control of the export and import of mining production, manufacturing, agriculture, and cattle. For example, land access to the port of Bilbao was fundamental for the city's development and great economic growth. Through time, Bilbao has acquired a dominant position with respect to other ports (such as Bermeo, Lekeitio, and Castro), becoming the predominant outlet for autochthonous products, princi-

Cut in half
One significant factor in the configuration of the Basque infrastructural network has been the Franco-Spanish state border, which has separated the country into two realities in terms of transportation infrastructures.
Map by Jennifer Thermes.

---

pally iron ore, and the exports (and imports) of a large part of the Castilian Meseta (wool) and the Upper Ebro Valley. In the nineteenth century it became the point of entry for British and Asturian coal and of exit for the primary derivatives of Bizkaian siderurgy. Land access by road and, later, railway would be definitively strategic for Bilbao. When different regions or districts had quick, direct access to its port, Bilbao reaped the benefits.

Trade relations and mercantile traffic have therefore configured a historical moment of the development of transportation infrastructures, the extension of roads and railways, and the enlargement of ports. This impetus, which extends into the present, was reinforced by a late-nineteenth-century Basque industrialization promoted by the high volume of traffic with Great Britain and the rest of Europe through Basque ports and the subsequent consolidation of the Bilbao area, mainly as an industrial and financial center within the Spanish market. When economic development extended throughout the country, the infrastructural network became more densely connected, reaching the far corners of Basque geography.

ON THE OTHER hand, one significant factor in the configuration of the Basque infrastructural network has been the Franco-Spanish state border, which has separated the country into two realities in terms of transportation infrastructures, and continues to do so. This border has been reinforced with the development of "national" markets since the nineteenth century. It has been an obstacle to communications between the Northern and Southern Basque Country, with both connected to their respective state markets. The situation changed with Spain's integration into the European Community and the creation of the European Internal Market, which will require a network of roads that takes this new reality into consideration.

AN OVERVIEW OF THE BASQUE INFRASTRUCTURAL NETWORK

At present, the Basque infrastructural network falls under the jurisdiction of different administrations. This creates the need for coordination between them when designing, developing, and managing the network. However, the current institutional framework, which divides the Basque territory into three administrative realities (the BAC, the FCN, and a Northern Basque Country that lacks its own institutional framework), has discouraged cooperation or earnest collaboration, frequently out of purely politic interest. Moreover, in the case of the BAC, some of the administrative control in such matters belongs to the Foral Deputations. Only permanent cooperation among the various institutions, therefore, can guarantee the compatibility of priorities and rhythms of different projects that will, in turn, ensure the development of a coherent network.

THE NETWORK OF ROADS

A crossroads of sorts, the Basque Country joins the north-south, Irun-Madrid route with the east-west, Barcelona-Zaragoza corridor to the northern Spanish coast. The Basque Country is bisected by N-1, which forms part of the first-class E-5 European route; N-1, A-8 (E-70), and A-68 (E-80) are the Iberian Peninsula's main links with the rest of Europe.

THE NETWORK OF roads plays the double function of internal and external connection. Without going into great depth, an overview, including some of the more relevant projects, can be provided.

Four categories, in some cases not mutually exclusive, can be distinguished:
1. International routes that connect with the European continent and act as a north-south vertebral axis: N-1 (Madrid-Irun); the connection project to increase capacity between the A-8 expressway (Bilbao-Behobia) and A-68 (Bilbao-Zaragoza); and the Eibar/Vitoria-Gasteiz expressway project.

2. Connections of the Basque Country with the main state centers and nearby regions: the Cantabrian two-lane highway along the northern Spanish coast; N-1, the main route to Madrid; the Bilbao-Zaragoza A-68 expressway, which connects with the Mediterranean axis (Barcelona); and the connection of Labourd's coast (Bayonne-Anglet-Biarritz) with Bordeaux and Paris (A-63) and Pau (A-64).
3. Intraregional roads, whose main function is the internal cohesion of the country: it is composed of several expressways and two-lane highways. Some have already been mentioned; others include the Navarre-Gipuzkoa (Leizaran) two-lane highway; the Sakana two-lane highway (N-1); the Altsasu-Irurtzun-Pamplona expressway connecting Vitoria-Gasteiz with Pamplona; the Eibar/Vitoria-Gasteiz expressway project; and the Durango-Bergara-Beasain two-lane highway project (whose building will fortify the scarcely connected west-east axis).
4. District and local roads: they provide the network with density; they favor the interconnection between neighboring districts and municipalities and contribute to accessibility across the entire territory.

Transportation within the Basque Country is therefore developing through a dense network of roads, with multiple access routes to the territorial capitals and larger towns.

THE RAILWAY NETWORK

The Basque Country is linked to all the most important Spanish cities by the RENFE (Spanish Rail) network. Basque rail communications also include the FEVE and EuskoTren networks. The former covers most of northern Spain; the latter, owned by the Basque government, provides local and suburban services for the three Basque capitals.

The BAC's rail network has 563 kilometers of track. One of the most important lines runs from Miranda to Irun (part of the Madrid-Paris line); the other, from Bilbao to Miranda (connecting Bizkaia with the Spanish meseta). A recent addition is the Bilbao Metro, which provides the city's inhabitants with fast, reliable service within the metropolitan Bilbao area.

THE BASQUE COUNTRY is currently preparing to tackle one of the most important rail projects ever undertaken in the region. The "Basque Y" will eventually provide all three BAC capital cities with high-speed links to the rest of Spain and Portugal and to the European high-speed network. Under the new layout, the stretch between Vitoria-Gasteiz and the French border is considered part of the key European Vitoria-Dax link, meaning that it will be built with European funds. The Vitoria-Gasteiz/Bilbao branch line is included in the Spanish General Plan on Infrastructures.

With investments surpassing 400 billion pesetas, the future European-gauge (1.45 meters) rail connection between the three BAC capitals will cover 165 kilometers in all, and 55% of the new line will be underground.

THE PORTS

The two leading trading ports of the Southern Basque Country are Bilbao and Pasaia. At the dawn of the twenty-first century, both are undergoing far-reaching changes in both management and facilities as major arrival and departure points for petroleum products, general merchandise, vehicles, and steel. The ultimate aim of the strategic plans being implemented by their directors is to increase the added value of their commer-

To accommodate trade, roads and railways were extended and ports enlarged. Basque industrialization in the late nineteenth-century created a high volume of traffic with Great Britain and the rest of Europe. *Engraving from Harold Hart:* The Illustrator's Handbook.

cial operations by enlarging facilities and diversifying traffic.

THE PORTS OF Bilbao and Pasaia are among Spain's leading trading ports, with a combined cargo throughput of around thirty million tons a year.

The Southern Basque Country also has fifteen smaller ports of varying sizes handling cargo, fishing, and leisure crafts. Most have enlarged their wharves and surface areas to meet increased requirements. An example is Bermeo, which has become a trading port again while retaining its importance as a fishing port.

The Port of Bayonne (Northern Basque Country) plays a major role in local economic development. Most of its trade comes from corn, metallurgical products, sulfur, and oil products. In 1998, the port, with 4.3 million tons of trade, crossed the symbolic barrier of four million tons for the second consecutive year, thus confirming its position as France's ninth most active seaport. A thousand ships have visited the port.

THE AIRPORTS

The Basque Country also has five airports—Bilbao (Sondika), Vitoria-Gasteiz (Foronda), San Sebastian (Hondarribia), Pamplona (Noain), and Biarritz, one in each territory (except for Soule)—that combine to provide full service. The four airports in the Southern Basque Country provide services that complement each other: international and domestic passenger flights use Sondika, charter and interregional flights use Foronda, and Hondarribia and Noain both service domestic flights within Spain. In 1998, more than 2.5 million passengers and 60,000 aircraft passed through these four airports.

THE PROGRESSIVE increase in air traffic and forecasts for the near future have led to an important investment program aimed at enlarging the airports and improving facilities. Daily links are available from the Bayonne-Anglet-Biarritz airport to Paris, London, and many provincial French cities. In 1999, nearly 800,000 passengers were transported. As already discussed, the Basque Country is currently working on a number of projects to modernize its transportation even more. Among the most important of these initiatives are the new high-speed rail line (known as the Basque Y), extension work on the port of Bilbao and the Bilbao airport, and a whole series of major projects included in the Euskadi 2000Tres Plan recently created by the Basque government.

PROBLEMS AND CHALLENGES FOR THE FUTURE

The infrastructural and transportation policy and urban and regional policies throughout the Basque Country have generated several problems, with the following being the most noteworthy:

1. Excessive spatial concentration of economic activities, employment, public administrations, cultural activities, transportation, and so on has given rise to agglomeration diseconomies in more and more metropolitan and urban areas, with an especially great impact on Bilbao and San Sebastian and their respective surroundings. Among the consequences are pollution and environmental damage, congestion (population, traffic, and so on), lower quality of life, and increased cost for business expansion.
2. A decrease is noticeable in the mobility of goods, services, and citizens in certain areas, affected by congestion problems and peripheral localization. Access to and from some places is clearly limited and problematic, creating excessive economic and social costs and a loss of opportunities to attract new activities and employment.
3. The construction of large infrastructural networks requires great investment within a very short period of time. Moreover, the amount of money necessary for construction and infrastructure upkeep is rising significantly. Such high expenditure has configured the future of Basque society by absorbing resources that could be used in other sectors and for other social needs.

4. The existing institutional and jurisdictional framework conditioned the infrastructural and transportation policy that could be implemented by a particular administration. In addition, several administrations are frequently involved, thus complicating the decision-making process, financing, management, and so on.
5. The process of undertaking an infrastructural project suffers from a degree of democratic deficit in all phases (planning, design, decision, evaluation, management, and inspection). Real, active participation of all social and economic agents would enhance the process, eliminate the conflict that frequently arises, and provide social legitimacy to such projects and to infrastructural policy in general.

Lesson thirteen

BIBLIOGRAPHY

Basque Government.
    http://www.euskadi.net/infraestru/indice_i.htm.
Chambre de Commerce et d'Industrie de Bayonne Pay Basque.
    http://www.bayonne.cci.fr/english/frames_eng/transporter_eng.htm.
Gómez Uranga, M., and G. Etxebarria. 1993. "Networks and Spatial Dynamics: The Case of the Basque Country." *European Planning Studies* 1(3):299–319.
———. 1994. "Institutional Agreements and Long-term Infrastructure Finance Schemes." Challenges to Institutional and Evolutionary Economic Theory: Growth, Uncertainty and Change. EAEPE 1994 Conference, October 27–29.

Geography and infrastructure

LEARNING GOAL
Describe the historical evolution of the infrastructural networks in the Basque Country and characterize their present condition.

WRITTEN LESSON FOR SUBMISSION
1. How do the different means of transportation in the Basque Country complement or compete with each other?
2. What are the problems and challenges for the future in the field of Basque infrastructure?

14 · Agriculture
The Basque sector within the European Union

HISTORICAL EVOLUTION

The primary sector was always one of the main sources of production within the Basque Country until the massive industrialization process that took place in Bizkaia at the end of the nineteenth century. Industrialization would occur later in Gipuzkoa, and not until the midtwentieth century in the other two territories.

THIS CHAPTER deals with the evolution of the Southern Basque Country's four territories into the present. (The difficulties in this sector in the Northern Basque Country will be dealt with in separate chapters, due to the lack of comparative data.)

As will be seen in the chapter about the fishing sector, fishing is important on the coast, despite its decline in recent decades.

As shown in Table 14-1, the rise in value of production experienced by the sector in the 1960s was followed by a stagnant period with short-term ups and downs, but a clear overall downward trend. Production in 1995 did reach 1975 levels, showing that the sector's importance within the Basque productive structure is declining steadily. Similarly, in the last four decades, the gross added value has increased to 1.28 times its 1955 value, whereas it has multiplied by 4.4 in the rest of the productive sectors as a whole.

The Basque Country thus maintains its role as net importer in the primary sector as a whole. This is because its capacity for answering internal demand through its own primary sector production decreased to its lowest ever: 38% in 1995. Production in the primary sector has declined continuously throughout the

Table 14-1.
Gross added value (price of factors, constant billion pesetas, based on 1986)

	1955	1965	1975	1985	1991	1995	1997
FCN	26.141	39.027	36.953	37.816	42.597	35.008	36.920
Araba	4.613	8.949	10.018	9.409	12.526	9.008	10.113
Bizkaia	19.008	24.157	24.807	25.500	38.331	18.388	30.114
Gipuzkoa	22.128	28.729	27.813	23.295	22.884	29.869	19.028
Southern Basque Country	67.877	90.564	90.451	81.499	96.625	87.134	78.283

Source: Fundación BBV, 1999.

Table 14-2
Employment in the primary sector (number of people).

	1955	1965	1975	1985	1991	1995	1998
FCN	86,253	60,992	39,528	23,576	13,782	11,680	11,602
BAC	97,653	87,981	65,876	38,002	29,051	25,439	24,236
Araba	19,899	15,840	11,428	8,103	5,812	4,892	4,684
Bizkaia	48,616	44,528	28,800	17,045	13,549	12,432	11,860
Gipuzkoa	29,138	27,613	25,648	12,854	9,690	8,115	7,692
Southern Basque Country	183,906	148,973	105,404	61,578	42,833	37,119	35,838

Source: Fundación BBV.

Vertical husbandry
The rugged terrain in parts of the Basque Country makes farming difficult; 85% of useful agrarian land in the BAC is mountain farming area.
Cliffs from Gustave Doré's Death of Korah, Dathan, and Abiram. The cow is from Jim Harter: Animals.

decade, especially in the fishing sector, confirming its increasing dependence on external resources.

The number of people working in the primary sector has decreased in recent decades, and this trend continues. In 1998, the number of workers in this sector was 3.7% of the full-time employees in the Southern Basque Country (3.1% in the BAC and 5.5% in the FCN).

GEOGRAPHIC AND SECTORIAL DISTRIBUTION OF BASQUE AGRICULTURE

There are two clearly differentiated geographical areas in the Basque primary sector. The first one includes Bizkaia, Gipuzkoa, the north of the FCN, and Araba. Its production focuses predominantly on livestock and forests and, in the first two territories, fishing. The second area includes the remainder of Araba and the FCN. There, agriculture (cereals, potatoes for both consumption and planting, sugar beets, wine, fruit and vegetables) plays a larger role.

As seen in Table 14-3, the focus of production within the subsectors has changed. Livestock always predominated over agriculture in the Basque Country until the mid-1990s. Since then, the trend has reversed, with agriculture currently accounting for 34% of total production. In the Southern Basque Country, fishing and aquaculture (fish farming) accounted for 14.5% of the gross added value in 1998; farming and livestock, 85.5%. Thus, the majority of production within the sector is within farming and livestock, with the contribution from fish being much less.

Production in the timber sector has significantly increased in recent years for different reasons. On one hand, the steady rise in prices throughout the decade has encouraged an increase of fellings; on the other, the production cycle has prepared an important part of the

Table 14-3
Production of farm subsectors in the Southern Basque Country (%)

	1985*	1998*
Agricultural production	43.7	45.8
Livestock production	47.5	40.7
Timber production	6.4	10.8

* The rest is in other activities.
Source: 1985: Banco de Bilbao, 1998: Caja Laboral.

timber mass for fellage. The most important species, the radiata pine, was widely reforested between 1957 and 1966. In a normal, thirty-year cycle, they would have been ready for fellage around 1990 and 1995. The drought of the late 1980s, however, caused a plethora of fires, which in turn provoked a high number of fellings to deal with the burnt wood. This created a price decrease, discouraging owners from undertaking final fellage.

FROM 1992 onward, especially in the past few years, prices have been on the rise; furthermore, final fellage always increases the value of wood. Beginning in 2001, a sharp decline of the fellage was expected, again causing a relative decline of this sector (which accounted for 23% of total agricultural production in 1998).

THE AGRICULTURAL AND FISHING SECTOR
The importance of family businesses is one of the main characteristics of the sector, as is the high atomization of land property (that is, the small size of the farms in operation). According to the 1989 Agrarian Census, 53.3% of the farms in the BAC and 60% of those in the

FCN were of 5 hectares or less. There are, moreover, parts in the Basque Country where farming is particularly difficult because the uniquely rugged terrain creates harsh conditions on the mountains and underpriviledged areas. In the BAC, 85% of the useful agrarian land (SAU) is considered mountain farming area; the percentage is lower in the FCN.

Furthermore, a significant aging of the sector's workforce and a great gap between the services offered in rural areas and those needed go hand in hand with the decline.

This sector, however, does have great potential, including the farming population's high level of qualification, the high degree of cooperation in some venues, and the ever higher tendency to join associations. A significant percentage of farmers belong to EHNE-UAGA (a union of Araban farmers and livestock breeders), followed by UAGN (a union of Navarrese farmers and livestock breeders) and ENBA. The growing concern for quality, "designation of origin" quality authentication, and respect for the environment offer the possibility of producing higher quality goods for an increasingly demanding market.

AT PRESENT, around twenty products in this sector are included within the "designation of origin" category by the BAC or Navarre. Involvement in this sector is growing and bringing about qualitative changes. This kind of production encourages producers to join forces, thus concentrating supply and promoting quality and the high standard demanded by consumers.

In the case of the FCN, good agricultural assistance services are available through the Technical Institutes of Management (ITG) created in 1980 by the territory's government. These were initially provided on a case-by-case basis, but later extended to the entire sector through the ITG for agriculture and the ITG for livestock breeding.

THE INFLUENCE OF EU AGRICULTURAL POLICIES (CAP)
Spain's entry into the EU has had a decisive influence on the sector's evolution. Transnationally, the agricultural sector is regulated by a Common Agrarian Policy (CAP)—the first true community policy in the European Economic Community and the leading recipient within the community budget for decades. Some years, it has used nearly three quarters of the budget; it currently uses about half.

AT THE TIME OF the policy's creation, Europe suffered from an agricultural shortage as a consequence of the war years. The resulting proproduction orientation to the land gave rise to a surplus of those products under its control, creating an imbalance in both the community budget and international trade. The CAP reacted by establishing a quota system, which began with the 1984 milk quota.

The CAP engages in community funding of the agricultural sector through the European Fund for Agriculture Guidance and Guarantee, with the Guarantee section being the one that administers the largest part—90%—of the agriculture budget. The fund is a vehicle imbued with the philosophy of the CAP about the different sectors and agriculture activities, allowing the CAP to provide different levels of support to the different goods produced in Europe. The result is a geographic inequality and high concentration of subsidies. In the early 1990s, 20% of the farmers received 80% of the community financing, while it is estimated that 4% of the farmers currently receive 40% of the subsidies. The 1992 reform tried to overcome the imbalance and inequalities caused by the CAP. This reform attempted

Woodcutter
In Bizkaia and Gipuzkoa the main tree species is the radiata pine that was widely reforested between 1957 and 1966. In Araba and Navarra, instead, old-growth species are still important.
Engraving by the school of Thomas Bewick.

---

to resolve the problem of surplus and its budget cost and defended (at least in theory) the multifunctional nature of the rural environment. It therefore included direct subsidies to farmers and compensation for leaving the profession. The problems remained unsolved, however, and the CAP therefore had to be revised in 1994 and 1999. These reforms have nevertheless not managed to change the operating methods or structure of EU subsidies, which continue to propagate territorial and sectorial inequalities.

This is why, at the time of Spain's 1986 inclusion, the EEC was in the midst of a reform process to confront such inequalities. This combined with poor negotiation by the Spanish administration to have a very negative impact on the sector. The EU's clear design to make Spain into a consumer of surpluses rather than a producer is exemplified by the milk quota. The production quota designated in the mid-1980s for Spain was a million tons under its actual production, and two million under what it needed for its own internal consumption. The impact on the Basque agricultural sector, consisting of small, largely unproductive farms, has also been very negative.

THE LOWER LEVEL of subsidies to the BAC and the FCN is marked. The former appears to be losing out because of its low output. Production is noticeably higher in Navarre, especially after the 1992 reform. Farm subsidies in Navarre actually increased from 1% of the Final Agricultural Production (PFA) in 1982 to 17% in 1994. This means that 25.7% of agricultural income comes from subsidies, indicating sectorial overdependence on EU policy and vulnerability to its changes. Furthermore, the encouragment of farmers to leave the profession rather than the renewal of agricultural resources combines with extreme limits on production to contribute to the instability of a sector whose future remains uncertain after fifteen years.

Spain's entry into the EU had a direct impact on the BAC and FCN's loss of control over the agricultural sector; exclusive control had been granted them by the autonomy statutes a few years earlier. EU membership, however, empowered the state as the sole negotiator of the community agreements in such matters, with unfavorable consequences for BAC and FCN alike.

Finally, it should be emphasized that the agricultural industry is very important to the primary sector and its profitability. It constitutes one part of the industrial sector and will be revisited in the chapter devoted to industry.

Lesson fourteen

BIBLIOGRAPHY
Eusko Ikaskuntza. http://www.euskonews.com.
EHNE. http://www.ehne.org.

LEARNING GOALS
1. Show the weight and evolution of this sector within the productive structure of the Basque economy.
2. Outline the geographic and sectorial distribution of Basque agriculture.
3. Identify the impact of entry into the European Union on this sector.

WRITTEN LESSON FOR SUBMISSION
1. Search the relevant websites and describe the main aims and services offered by the principal Basque agricultural trade unions to their members.
2. Analyze the principal effects of entry into the European Union on the agricultural sector in the Basque Country.

15 · The Basque fishing sector
A Brief History

THE FISHING SECTOR has long-standing importance in the Basque economy. Basques are believed to have been the first whale-hunting experts. They began their transatlantic adventures in the sixteenth century, spending long months off the Terranova coast to hunt whales and fish for cod. This tradition began to decline in the eighteenth century, when England seized those fishing waters.

Fishing out of Gipuzkoan ports therefore decreased, but it remained steady on the Bizkaian coast. Labourd's fishing focused on species to be canned. Canning spread to the Southern Basque Country in the second half of the nineteenth century, thereby providing jobs—especially for women.

By century's end, technological innovations related to ships (steam engines, greater hold, and so on) and fishing tackle (trawl line) were responsible for overfishing both internationally and locally. This trend became increasingly pronounced, resulting in falling catches.

Throughout the twentieth century, the ups and downs in Basque fishing have mirrored those in the sector on an international level. A downward trend in the evolution of catch per fishing production unit is apparent, the result of overfishing by industrialized countries. The 1960s, however, witnessed a general increase in capacity under the Law for the Renewal of the Fishing Fleet, with the Basque sector also positively affected. Advantageous loans were provided to increase the capacity of the Basque fleet, but it would subsequently outgrow sectorial capacity and get heavily into debt.

CRISIS AND THE REORGANIZATION OF THE BASQUE FISHING SECTOR WITHIN THE EUROPEAN FRAMEWORK From 1975 onwards, the establishment of Exclusive Economic Areas of 200 miles limited the possibilities of the fishing fleet. In 1982, the Common Fishing Policy (CFP) was initiated on the European level. The focus of this policy was to guard against overfishing, while still ensuring fishing livelihoods and reasonable prices for both consumers and the canning industry. Some annual admissible total catch (ATC) rates, applicable to some species vital to the EEC fleets, were therefore established. Each ATC is distributed yearly among the member states through quotas (which are not always respected). The European Union does recognize the insufficiency of the measures and the necessity to combat excess fishing.

THE BASQUE fishing sector became subject to this set of regulations as a result of Spain's 1986 entry into the then-EEC. Spain's assigned quota brought about a great reduction in fishing. Furthermore, because the share coefficients assigned to other member states were not altered after its entry, Spain was placed under a "special system" clearly disadvantageous for the Basque fleet, especially for deep-sea fishing. The 1992 CFP reform did not bring any significant changes to the system, which remains valid until December 31, 2002.

Beginning in 2000, the European Union's decision to declare a 52% reduction in the quota on anchovy (the highest-priced species) for reasons of preservation had a significant impact on the Basque fleet's spring coastal fishing. Meanwhile, French fishers are allowed to use pelagic trawl lines—a constant source of dispute between the two fleets, due to the havoc they cause. In addition, in spite of the overall reduction of quotas and an off-season in one part of French fishing waters

Basques are believed to have been the first whale-hunting experts. They began their transatlantic adventures in the sixteenth century, spending long months off the Terranova coast to hunt whales and fish for cod.
Engraving from Jim Harter: Animals.

(between Bayonne and Bordeaux), the French fleet has been granted permission to catch the quota assigned to Portugal in the Bay of Biscay. This has broken the agreements between the two fleets, by which the Basque fleet relinquished part of its EU-assigned quota to the French and in return the French trawl liners waited until the anchovy season was over.

WITH THE REDUCTION of the quota, the Basque fishermen cannot supply the 9,000 tons of anchovy they offered as compensation. The Basques have therefore offered to discontinue the legal action they had started against the transfer of the Portuguese quota rights to the French, if the French stop fishing with pelagic trawl liners south of La Rochelle. The fragility of the agreements and the problems concerning the quota system are prevalent in current events. Moreover, in June, there was a revision of the quota system in which the studies carried out by AZTI (a public company run by the Basque government) were taken into account.

THE BASQUES have been against tuna limits, provided that the historical fishing operation of its fleet is respected. The only existing international regulation, not implemented by the European Commission, concerns the number of ships. The type of fishing tackle used for catching tuna has been another of the main problems. While Basque fishermen use live bait, the French use nets that float adrift for several kilometers and catch a variety of species. In 1997, an agreement forbidding the use of such nets in 2002 was reached, in spite of French opposition.

To date, only Spanish delegates have taken part in these negotiations, Basque representatives having been denied a voice. Many jurisdictional conflicts have therefore arisen between the two administrations. Although the state had relinquished exclusive jurisdiction over fishing policy to the BAC in the 1979 Statute of Autonomy, Spain's entry into the European Community placed fishing under Spanish governmental control. The positions defended by the central government in European fora are not previously negotiated with the representatives of the BAC or other autonomous communities on the coast.

In conclusion, crisis and reorganization are the two main features of the Basque fishing sector. These trends are unfolding within a context of gradual reduction of fishing within the EU, meticulously complied with by some states, like Spain, but not others. The problems affecting the sector are pervasive and varied. They range from sea pollution to discard problems (some seasons, such as spawning, the catch of unacceptable fish relative to acceptable ones increases). Moreover, the unwillingness of the states to inspect fishing tackle, the off-seasons, and salary control of people working in this sector make it impossible to abandon an exclusively profit-based view of marine resources.

THE CURRENT SITUATION
Fishing currently accounts for a low rate of the BAC's gross domestic product and workforce—approximately 1% in both cases. This is the consequence of the sector-wide crisis and reorganization of recent decades; as seen in Table 15-1, the numbers of ships and jobs have decreased. The sector nevertheless remains important. RATES ARE comparable to those in other countries, and the Basque fleets rank fourth within the European Union. In addition, the sector's importance is concentrated geographically in fishing towns, whose life largely depends on fishing. Each direct job in catching fish is estimated to create an average of four indirect jobs. Nevertheless, the sector is undergoing difficulties, as will be discussed later. Young people are generally unwilling to embark on such a career because of the poor working conditions at present.

Coastal and deep-sea fishing are distinguished as subsectors, with the former being more important. Coastal fishing is done a few miles offshore and has two main seasons: spring, when anchovy is the principal catch, and summer, when tuna is fished. The two combined to account for 66.5% of the total catch and 89.14% of income in 1992. This dependence is a weakness that results in a low usage of ships.

Deep-sea fishing is done beyond the Bay of Biscay. The most important subgroup by volume is the catch of

Table 15-1
Ships, jobs, and gross registered tonnage (GRT) of the Basque fishing sector

	Number of ships		Employment		GRT	
Year	87	97	87	97	87	97
Coastal	535	366	4,204	2,723	64,083	18,959
Deep sea	215	108	3,889	1,874	90,748	53,008
Total	750	474	8,090	4,597	154,831	71,967

Source: Caja Laboral, "Basque Economy" (1987 and 1998 Yearbooks).

---

fresh fish, with hake the most prized. The next subgroup is the tuna freezer ships. Geographically concentrated in the port of Bermeo (Bizkaia), they constitute the most modern and profitable part of the Basque fleet.

THE BASQUE GOVERNMENT'S PARTICIPATION IN THE SECTOR

The BAC government has developed policies targeting this sector. In 1994, it created a Fishing Strategic Plan (PEP) that will be in effect until 2003. The Fishing Forum has also begun to function as the meeting point for all agents and activities related to the fishing sector.

WITH RESPECT TO the PEP, it has various objectives including the renewal, modernization, and structural adjustment of both the fleet and fishing techniques. Special emphasis is placed on research, carried out by AZTI.

The BAC is the only autonomous community in Spain that has cofinanced the approved programs for dismantling its own ships with the European Union and the central state government. In this sense, the reorganization of the Basque fishing sector is considered to have come to an end in 1997. Due to recent legislative changes in EU regulations, the fleet's modernization and replacement are currently being undertaken with public funds. Subsidies for replacing the fleet were negligible until 1999, especially when compared to those given other regions. But with the new Renewal Plan, thirty-seven new ships were built in 1999—as many as in the previous five years combined. Moreover, the problem will be solved between 2000 and 2006, since the Basque government will be allowed to finance 50% of the cost of shipbuilding.

IN CONCLUSION, overfishing continues throughout the world, making the future of the sector highly problematic. The Basque fishing sector is especially riddled with uncertainty and risks, since it is not represented in the decision-making fora. Nevertheless, the potential of the sector, its long tradition, and the renewal of the fleet all must be taken into account. The negotiations of the Common Fishing Policy in 2002 therefore represent a decisive challenge for the near future of the Basque fishing fleet.

Lesson fifteen

BIBLIOGRAPHY

Astorkiza, K., I. Astorkiza, and I. del Valle. 1998. "Fisheries Policy and the Cofradias in the Basque Country: The Case of Albacore and Anchovy." Working Papers, Public University of Navarre, Pamplona.

AZTI. http://www.azti.es.

Eusko Ikaskuntza. http://www.euskonews.com.

Lucio, P, and I. Artetxe. 1997. "Notes on deep sea fisheries in the Basque Country." Sukarrieta: AZTI.

LEARNING GOALS

1. Explain the course of evolution of the fishing sector in the Basque Country.
2. Describe the main characteristics of the European Union's Common Fishing Policy and its effects on the Basque fleet.
3. Discuss the most important problems the sector has to face in the near future.

WRITTEN LESSON FOR SUBMISSION

Search the website of the European Union for the primary changes that the Common Fishing Policy will probably face in the near future. Give your opinion on the impact the policy will have on the Basque fleet.

16 · Geography of industry
The Basque Autonomous Community

As has been the case in neighboring countries, industry in the BAC has been losing ground in its total gross added value. According to the input-output tables it has fallen from 39.7% in 1985 to 32.9% in 1995.

Nevertheless, the BAC is still a predominantly industrial region with a degree of specialization above that of surrounding countries. The external coverage rate remains more than 100, meaning that the BAC is a net exporter of industrial goods.

However, industry in the BAC is not free from problems. The manufacturing sector is a relatively poor generator of added value; in 1995, only 37.5% of the distributed production of the sector was in added value. The following pages will argue that the manufacturing industry's specialization and concentration are the possible source of the problem. First, however, the evolution of industry in the BAC during the recovery period that began in 1985 will be addressed.

EVOLUTION OF INDUSTRY IN THE BAC SINCE 1985
Beginning in 1985, accompanying the international expansive cycle, the Basque economy underwent a remarkable recovery as a result of increased capital-goods investment. From 1985 to 1990, Basque industry experienced an average annual accumulative growth rate of 4.7% in gross added value (market prices), in real terms.

As a result of the recession between 1991 and 1993, Basque industry's GAV experienced a negative growth of 4.7%, accompanied by a 12% decline in industrial jobs.

From 1994 until the end of 2000, the Basque economy experienced an upsurge, with industry playing a critical role, though in 2001 the trend changed due to the international economic decline. A tremendous upsurge in external demand (especially within the EU), demand within Spain, and a resurgence in capital-goods investment have been the primary reasons. The industrial workforce, which had fallen to 195,000 in 1994, rose to 240,000 in 1998. This number, however, remains below the 275,000 employed in the sector in 1985.

The results for Basque business agree with these trends. The second half of the 1980s witnessed a marked improvement in the economic-financial indicators of the BAC's manufacturing industry. The structure of business costs improved, debt was cancelled, and costs reduced, all providing relief from the burdens of the earlier crisis.

Between 1990 and 1993, however, the structure of costs and the financial balance deteriorated, becoming especially acute in the latter year. This recession exceeded that suffered by European industry. The weakness of Basque industrial structure stands out; in moments of crisis, Basque industries tend to be less financially adaptable than their European competitors.

FROM 1994 ONWARD, together with the change of cycle on the international level, business has once again improved. Among the factors that influenced the Basque economy very strongly during this period have been: the reduction of financing costs (the converging interest rates in the European Community), the devaluation of the peseta from 1992 onward (after its notorious overvaluation from 1988 to 1992), the deregulation of the electrical sector, and ports.

Despite this recent recovery, the structural problems that surfaced between 1990 and 1993 demonstrate that

Basque industry has yet to be fully consolidated. Some areas for improvement of the BAC's manufacturing industry are therefore broached in the next section.

SPECIALIZATION OF THE MANUFACTURING INDUSTRY IN THE BAC

The manufacturing industry in the BAC remains highly specialized in certain sectors. This does not in itself necessarily constitute a problem. Successful highly specialized economies do exist, because specialization can be to the benefit of economies of specialization and conglomeration due to a region's tradition of efficiency.

Nevertheless, some authors argue that the problems lie in the characteristics intrinsic to the sectors in which Basque industry is specialized. They claim that industry in the BAC is concentrated in sectors that are regressive—low in technological level, slow in demand growth, low in productivity, and so on. Relatedly, progressive sectors account for a low percentage of Basque industry.

This scheme will be followed here, although caution must be taken not to overgeneralize. In fact, more thorough analyses are needed, from both sectorial and business perspectives, to dispel misguided stereotypes about particular sectors. For example, despite assertions to the contrary, the steel industry should not be considered outdated or on the decline.

THE CONCEPT OF relative specialization will be employed here. A country or region is considered relatively specialized in one sector when the rate of gross added value (GAV) of that sector with respect to that country or region's total GAV is higher than the normal rate in the same sector in other developed countries (such as those in the EU, the United States, and Japan), used as a frame of reference.

The English industrial revolution promoted the development of capitalism and a new industrial society.
Engraving from Johann George Heck: Pictorial Archive of Nature & Science.

ANALYSIS BY PRODUCTION SECTIONS
In comparison to Spain and other industrialized states, BAC manufacturing is relatively specialized in intermediate goods. Its relative specialization in capital goods is higher than in Spain and comparable to those in leading developed countries. On the other hand, the BAC suffers from low specialization in the production of consumer

goods, suggesting a lack of coherence or structure in the Basque industrial sector.

The role of production in the generation and diffusion of new technologies throughout the entire industrial framework appears to bode well for BAC industry. That the level of production of capital goods is on par with developed countries may create excessive initial optimism. As discussed later, the technological level of Basque industry is not high enough. This could be the result of the specific content of the Basque capital-goods sector. The most significant companies in this sector are: Mecánica de la Peña, the Asea Brown Boveri (ABB) group, Construcciones y Auxiliar de Ferrocarriles (CAF), and Babcock Wilcox. This last one is the biggest, with annual sales of 51 billion pesetas. Some, such as Mecánica de la Peña and Babcock Wilcox, were undergoing difficulties in 2000.

ANALYSIS BY SECTORS OR BRANCHES OF PRODUCTION

The analysis of branches of production can be used to detect the industrial sectors in which the BAC is specialized. According to the input-output tables for 1995, the leading branches by their GAV of the industrial total would be steel and metal goods (30.70%); machinery (11.74%); oil refinement (8.10%); food, drinks, and tobacco (7.83%); rubber and plastics (7.76%); and transportation material (7.43%).

THESE RATES, however, must be supplemented with an analysis of the relative specialization. Compared to Spain and other industrialized states, the BAC is relatively specialized in steel and metal goods, machinery, and rubber and plastics. In this sense, the Basque iron and steel tradition has been important. In addition, the Basque machine tool, closely linked to Basque cooperatives, is fifth in the European rankings and ninth in the world. But considering the productive branches they occupy, industrial businesses are very small in the BAC.

On the other hand, other sectors such as food, drinks, and tobacco, or transportation material, are not relatively specialized in the BAC, in spite of their importance in the Basque industrial GAV.

SPECIALIZATION is great in the branches mentioned because the BAC's manufacturing industry in other branches is relatively undiversified. Recent years have brought an increase in the importance of interesting progressive branches, such as aeronautics and electrical machinery. In the aeronautics field there are companies like Gamesa, Industria de Turbopropulsores (ITP), and Sener. In any case, such new activity has generally been lacking in Basque industry.

BAC industry will now be analyzed in terms of technology and demand. Regarding technology, production of the manufacturing industry of the BAC would rate rather low in terms of relative specialization. Basque industrial production also lags behind in advanced technological specialization; this is so despite the significant progress made by the technologically high-level sectors, which nearly doubled their percentage within gross industrial production for manufactures, rising from 4.9% in 1985 to 8.3% in 1995 (data from the input-output tables). This importance, however, appears to be at the expense of the sectors with a median level of technology, since the rate for those with a low level remains the same. Although technological specialization seems superior in the Spanish economy, the Basque economy's investment in R&D (research and development) relative to GDP surpasses that of the Spanish economy.

In terms of demand, the manufacturing industrial sector of the BAC is relatively specialized in the slow-growth segment, not very specialized in the median segment, and depressed in the rapid-growth segment.

In conclusion, industry in the BAC is still highly specialized in regressive sectors. Nevertheless, as already noted, while this analysis offers a helpful guide, more thorough study is required. According to such criteria, for example, iron and steel would be considered a regressive and outdated sector, with a low level of technology and demand growth. This is not true, however.

THE TECHNOLOGICAL impetus of the sector is remarkable. It is underrepresented in the figures because the companies running minimills do not do research directly, but they do adopt the constant improvements introduced by engineering companies. Demand is also sufficiently high to make the sector profitable.

Lesson sixteen

BIBLIOGRAPHY

Basque Government. http://www.euskadi.net.
———. 1995. The Basque Country Department of Trade and Industry and the Institution of Electrical Engineers. Gobierno Vasco.
EVE. http://www.eve.es.
SPRI. http://www.spri.es.

LEARNING GOALS
1. Describe the evolution of industry in the region during the past few decades.
2. Portray the features, level of specialization, and concentration of Basque manufacturing.
3. Discuss the technological level of Basque industry.

WRITTEN LESSON FOR SUBMISSION
1. Has there been a great change in specialization of the branches of industry from the beginnings of industrialization in the region up to the present?
2. Searching the EUSTAT website, compare and contrast the main figures of the last few decades, from the major crisis of the 1970s to the late 1990s.

17 · Technology and innovation policy
The Basque Autonomous Community

THE INDUSTRIALIZATION process began in this part of the Basque Country in the second half of the nineteenth century. Its cradle was Bilbao, where iron mines were operated on a large scale by both foreign and local companies. These products were exported to big European iron and steel industries, mostly British. Some of the profits were subsequently reinvested in the Basque Country in iron and steel and other (mostly related) industries, such as shipyards, shipping firms, and the electrical, chemical, and paper industries. The financial sector also became very influential within the Spanish economy.

Until the mid-1970s, these were the main industries in the BAC, which was therefore highly specialized around steel and its related industries. When the international crisis hit the region, the impact was therefore great. Industrial jobs were steadily lost during the first half of the 1980s—100,000 jobs disappeared within a mid-1970s active population of 600,000. Industry thus declined from 54.6% of the GDP to 46.3%.

MAIN CHARACTERISTICS OF THE TECHNOLOGY POLICIES IMPLEMENTED DURING THE PAST TWO DECADES
In the context of crisis and lack of local investors at the end of the 1970s, in 1981, the Basque authorities set up a regional development agency, called the Agency for Industrial Promotion and Restructuring (SPRI), dependent on the Basque government. The agency's main aims were the promotion and restructuring of Basque industry, and its priority was to defend existing jobs and create new ones.

During SPRI's initial years, the Basque government's main industrial policy initiatives through the agency consisted in providing aid (basically subsidies and loans) to SMCs, or small and midsize companies (restructuring of large companies was controlled by the state government), which were experiencing great difficulties and were in danger of closing. Financial assistance was provided on a case-by-case basis, with no criteria by sectors, until the early 1990s. Thereafter, different plans were made, with the Monitor Company (run by Michael Porter) especially influential in establishing the BAC's main competitive sectors.

In summary, technological policy can be divided onto two phases: the 1980s and the 1990s.

MAIN CHARACTERISTICS OF THE POLICIES IN THE 1980s

During the 1980s, the first aim was to promote the adoption of technology by Basque industry. Two priorities were therefore established:

1. To create a network of technology centers sponsored by the government
2. To support R&D departments within companies

TECHNOLOGY CENTERS were established on the foundations of small testing and service laboratories already run by industrial centers and training schools. They have become one of the main motors of the autonomous community's R&D sector. The Department of Industry financed a significant amount of the research of such centers through "generic projects" created to collect and assimilate knowledge and technical skills in strategic fields in order to subsequently insert them into the Basque industrial framework.

The regional development agency used small subsidies to assist companies in launching research and development projects. This was called "seed" or "spread policy."
Drawing by G. Brian Karas

The second priority of this first technology policy was to support the R&D of companies. It was originally directed towards company R&D departments; later, some aid programs to company-based R&D projects were established. This was the beginning of the policy and its aim, without being selective, was to make companies sensitive to the need for R&D by giving them small subsidies (called "seed" or "spread policy").

In summary, a model of private technology transfer was chosen, but with a high level of public funding. This model was selected to provide the technical support necessary for private R&D. SMCs in particular were targeted, with SPRI transferring technology and providing support.

ONCE THE MEASURES were implemented, the need to control allocations and develop detailed planning policies was evident. In 1989, therefore, the Technologic Strategy Unit was created. It is a specific management unit designed to implement the technology policy of the Department of Industry. The unit designed a Plan for Technological Strategy, whereby new projects for strategic cooperation were established (directed to subjects selected within the main fields of the plan), evaluated by external experts, and proposed by groups formed by centers and companies. At the same time, the public funding of the technology centers was reduced for generic projects in order to push them to collaborate in individual and strategic projects with companies.

THE MAIN CHARACTERISTICS OF THE POLICIES IN THE 1990s

In the 1990s, industry and technology policy was redirected, based on the plans shown in Table 17-1.

In 1991, the First Comprehensive Industrial Policy Plan was drawn up. With it came a new phase of the technological policy, designed to adapt R&D infrastructure to meet company demand and to articulate this demand through the clusters. The weight of the clusters in the selection process of projects and partnerships therefore increased.

Table 17-1
The Basque Country: Evolution of economic policy in the 1990s

1990 Basque Country advantage: M. Porter and Monitor Consulting
1991 First Comprehensive Industrial Policy Plan
   1992: Clusters Program (6 Years)
   1993: Industrial Technology Plan: 1993–96 (First)
   1994: Energy Policy Plan: 1995–2000 (First)
1995 Second Comprehensive Industrial Policy Plan
   1997: Science and Technology Plan: 1997–2000 (Second)
   1997: Quality Policy Plan: 1997–2000 (Second)
   1998: Energy Policy Plan: 2000–05 (Second)

Thus, the Industrial Technology Plan 1993–96 took into account four kinds of projects:
1. One type of generic project (proposed by the technology centers).
2. A second type of generic project (proposed by the groups within the clusters or sectors and implemented by the technology centers or university departments). This was the first step toward including university research services within the generic projects.
3. Joint projects (between agents from both supply and demand sides of technology).
4. Individual projects (proposed by the companies).

THE MAIN technology areas at this time were information technology, new materials, manufacturing technologies, and those related to the environment. The main industrial sectors at this time were machine tools, automotive auxiliary industry, and information technologies.

In 1996, the Science and Technology Plan 1997–2000 was approved. In 1997, the Basque Technology Network was set up. Its aim was to incorporate all the agents (including the university) into the R&D infrastructure and coordinate their participation. A different level of public funding was established for each one.

THIS RECENT plan is believed to represent an important step, with the incorporation of the university into the R&D sector and the coordination of the science and technology policies of the Basque government. The plan has also maintained the priorities of strengthening R&D infrastructure, tailoring activities to technological demand, and prioritizing cooperation between companies.

The Science and Technology Plan 1997–2000 seeks to facilitate:

1. The new innovation model: technology, innovation, and training.
2. The development of a coordinated scientific-technological policy: experimental plan.
3. Technological supply and demand: through a shared-technology strategy, integrated projects, and full support to companies.
4. The structured consolidation of the technology supply: a new call for a proposal for the Basque technology network.
5. The process of incorporation of the university: joint work among education, industry, and the university.
6. The measurement of the results following a continuous improvement process.

INSTRUMENTS OF THE PLAN

Instruments of the plan include:

1. Infrastructure: Support for infrastructure is aimed at making business as a whole competitive and at developing human resources in the BAC. It includes activity involving the university, technology centers, technology parks, and the Innovation Relay Center.
2. R&D Projects: Support for R&D is fundamental for restructuring companies and promoting groups of particular interest at the university and technology centers. It is provided through projects to encourage cooperation, quality, and a market approach.
3. Technology Innovation: Support for structural change implies integrated support for technological innovation to ensure that, insofar as possible, efforts in science and technology development reach the market and society in general.
4. Training: Structural change is not possible without integrated training, ultimately focused on business requirements and provided through the value chain of scientist and technologist training, from the university to the technology centers, promoting the incorporation of individuals thus trained into businesses.

THE PROGRAMS of this plan provide basic guidelines for the previously listed instruments. They compose a set of priority technology lines and areas, most of which are designed to meet the needs of business in the BAC. The resources available to the Science and Technology Plan are limited, so priority must be given to areas where capability and experience are the poorest or where the possibilities for reaching a high international standard are greatest. In any event, the effort made in achieving true competitive advantages for the BAC in

Project
The Science and Technology Plan 1997-2000 incorporated the University of the Basque Country into the R&D infrastructure.
Illustration by Seymour Chwast.

---

the short, medium, and long term must be justified by results. The technology programs are ultimately designed to meet the requirements of the demand side of technology.

The programs[3] are classified as:

1. Basic Research Programs: Focused on basic scientific research. The main beneficiary will be the university, which will receive support for its research groups. The lines of research supported fall under the heading of the National R&D Plan and the EU Framework Program.
2. Horizontal Technology Programs: Bring together areas of general interest for the business sector as a whole, and more specific areas based on horizontal technologies. Such programs are guided by the current needs of companies in the BAC, thus ensuring that resources are used in areas where their effect on competitiveness will be greater. Priority technology areas for these programs are identified by looking at cluster technology plans, other areas of interest for business, and areas supported by supraregional programs.
3. Specific Technology Programs: Interdepartmental programs that coordinate the work of the Department of Industry with that of other technology-related Basque government departments. As with horizontal technology programs, they are guided by the current needs of the companies involved and the technology development and public investment programs of the different departments. Priority areas set by other, supraregional programs are also taken into account here.

In 2001, a new plan, the Science, Technology, and Innovation plan 2001–04, came into force and continues the goals of the previous plan. Its aim is to promote innovation in Basque enterprises in the areas of supply and demand and new technologies.

Lesson seventeen

BIBLIOGRAPHY
Basque Government. http://www.euskadi.net.
CDTI. http://www.cdti.es.
Cooke, P., and K. Morgan. 1997. *The Associated Economy: Firms, Regions and Innovation.* Oxford: Oxford University Press.
CSIC. http://www.csic.es.
Gómez Uranga, M., and G. Etxebarria. 2000. "Panorama of the Basque Country and Its Competence for Self-Government." *European Planning Studies* 8(4):521–535.
SPRI. http://www.spri.es.

LEARNING GOALS
1. Document the salient characteristics of the technology policies implemented by the regional government during the past two decades, including the main technology areas and industrial sectors promoted.
2. Discuss the features of the current plan, specifying its instruments and programs.

WRITTEN LESSON FOR SUBMISSION
Search the Basque government's website for information about the Science and Technology Plan for 1997–2000. Name the plan's main agents and list the instruments and projects in order of importance (as determined by their assigned budgets).

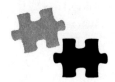

18 · Industry, innovation, perspectives
The Foral Community of Navarre

IN THE EARLY 1960s, Navarre was industrially underdeveloped. Its economy was based on traditional agriculture, which employed about 50% of the active population (Sodena, 1990) and generated 28% of the region's GAV in 1964. In less than fifty years, Navarre has experienced a great economic evolution. It is now one of the most prosperous industrial regions in Spain (Zabala, 1996).

Navarre's industrialization process accelerated in the 1960s, when some local entrepreneurs created large industries in various sectors, including machinery, metal products, automobile, and kitchen appliances. These growing industries employed all the surplus labor force from the agricultural sector and were the foundation for the first multinational companies that would later establish themselves in the region. They were also the source of young entrepreneurs who created new auxiliary firms (Sodena, 1998). It is remarkable that such industrial growth took place within a mere ten-year period.

Table 18-1 shows industry's importance in 1996. In Navarre, industry accounted for 43% of the GAV, above the Spanish and European average. The continuing significance of the agricultural sector in the region, however, is also noteworthy. Despite its decline, agriculture remains far above Spanish and European levels.

THE INDUSTRIAL FRAMEWORK

Navarre's industry is highly concentrated in a few sectors. In 2000, transportation and electrical materials accounted for 26.9% of the industrial GAV; metal products and machinery, about 20.4%; and food, drinks,

Table 18-1
Gross added value, Navarre, Spain, and EUR-15 (1996, %)

	Agriculture	Industry	Services
Navarre	6.0	43.5	50.5
Spain	3.7	33.2	63.1
EUR-15	2.3	30.7	67.0

Source: Own creation, with data from Eurostat and the government of Navarre.

Table 18-2
Gross added value, industrial sectors, Navarre (2000)

Energy products and water	5.2%
Transportation and electrical material	26.9%
Ore and siderometallurgy	7.2%
Food, drink, tobacco	11.8%
Nonmetal products	5.9%
Textile	2.1%
Chemical products	4.5%
Paper	8.2%
Metal products and machinery	20.4%
Plastics and wood	7.8%

Source: Creation of the Statistics Institute of Navarre's government, using data from the Industrial Enterprises Survey 2000 (INE, 2001).

Table 18-3
Number of companies in Navarre, by size (1998)

Employees	Companies	%
1–50	2,146	91.48
≤ 9	1,495	63.72
10–19	345	14.70
20–49	306	13.04
50–99	93	3.96
100–199	54	2.4
200–500	39	1.67
>500	14	0.59
Total	2,346	100

Source: Own creation, using data from DIRCE (INE, 1998).

and tobacco, about 12%. Nearly 60% of Navarre's industrial GAV was therefore produced in these three sectors alone.

IN 1998, THERE were 2,146 industrial companies, with more than 60% of them having nine employees or less. On the other hand, the number of large companies (of more than 500 employees) in such a small economy is noteworthy. In most cases, they are foreign capital companies.

REGIONAL INNOVATION POLICIES
The public sector has taken part in Navarre's industrial development since the beginnings of the process in the 1960s. All of its activity throughout the years has therefore focused on the promotion of private investment, creation of firms, discovery of new productive units, and so on. Its first foray into R&D would not be until 1982, when the Foral Parliament approved research and tech-

Technopark
The Technological Plan of Navarre 2000–2003 provides consultancy and training to SMEs about the new information and communication technologies.
Photograph: PhotoDisc, Inc.

---

nology development support regulation. The regulation established several guidelines for the promotion of such activities. Still in effect (having been renewed every year), this piece of legislation covers training for researchers, support for equipment infrastructure and instruments for research, assistance for R&D projects, funding for pilot plants, and support for the external sale of technology.

In 1991, the Research Regional Plan of Navarre (PRINA) (1992–95) was created. Among its objectives

Table 18-4
R&D expenditure out of total GDP (%)

	1987	1988	1989	1990	1991	1992	1993	1994	1995	1996
Navarre	51	35	45	88	93	98	92	74	81	83
Spain	64	72	75	85	87	91	91	85	85	87

Source: Own creation, using data from INE.

were to promote a research culture within the region that would give rise to high-level human capital and to encourage external financial participation in R&D programs to centers, associations, and R&D units established in Navarre. (For political reasons, the plan was never implemented.)

Navarre's government didn't approve a second plan for the region, the Technological Plan of Navarre 2000–2003, until March 1999. With this plan, the government aims to facilitate access to new technologies for the SMCs, provide financial support to entrepreneurial innovation initiatives, and promote technology centers and fields of innovation for the multinationals established in Navarre.

THE TECHNOLOGICAL Plan of Navarre 2000–2003 has a four-year budget of 19.937 billion pesetas. This plan is based on a supply-demand analysis of Navarre's needs. Its objective is to promote several lines that will improve the competitiveness of regional companies and increase employment by raising R&D expenditure from 0.9% to 1.6% of the GDP in the next four years. It will also try to triple business expenditure from 5.6 to 15.3 billion pesetas.

Several sectorial and thematic projects are planned in the Technological Plan of Navarre 2000–2003:

1. Automobile Experimental Center of Navarre, which will facilitate the retention and creation of advanced R&D departments in Navarre, not elsewhere (whether within Spain or not) (Gobierno de Navarra, 1999).
2. New information and communication technologies, whose main objective is to form SMCs and advise them about the new technologies.
3. Renewable Energy Technology Center of Spain, which will make the testing and demonstration of all renewable energy sources possible.
4. Applied Medicine Research Center, where the University of Navarre (UN) will combine basic research with a practical focus that will permit the transfer of results to clinics.
5. Innovation Park of Navarre, which will house companies, centers, and advanced technological services.
6. Incorporation of the new technologies into the equipment and machinery of the professional training centers.
7. Creation of the Agrobio-technology and Natural Resources Institute to promote the scientific development of the Public University of Navarre (UPNA).

R&D AGENTS

The latest statistical data available shows that the high percentages reached in Navarre at the beginning of the 1990s (higher than the Spanish average) have not been recovered. They are no longer above the Spanish average. In Tables 18-4 and 18-5, the most characteristic data of the R&D undertaken is clear.

TAKING R&D expenditure into account, the role of companies is the most important. At 55%, Navarre is above the Spanish average of 49%.

The second most active group in R&D expenditures is the higher education organizations. In Navarre, their

Suitable human
Since its foundation the University of Navarre has been devoted to the development of high-level human capital. It has been pivotal in the development of research activities in the region.
Photo: Illustrator's Reference Manual.

---

expenditures account for 41% of the total—well above the Spanish average of 32%. Likewise, in Navarre, university personnel represent 57% of the total employed in research.

THE UNIVERSITY of Navarre, privately founded in 1952, has been very involved in research from the outset, thus providing the region with a vital academic and research tradition. In 1986, the Scientific and

Table 18-5
R&D expenditure (billion pesetas) and full-time personnel (1997)

Navarre	R&D expenditure	%	Personnel	%
Companies*	5,677.49	54.6	665	39.5
Public administration	295.549	2.6	55	3.3
High education	4,430.02	41.4	964	57.2
Private institutions	1.414	1.4	1	0
Total sectors	10,404.47	100	1,685	100

Spain	R&D expenditure	%	Personnel	%
Companies*	327,922.13	48.8	30,022	34.4
Public administration	116,727.540	17.4	19,189	22
High education	219,950.85	32.7	36,843	42.3
Private institutions	7,416.14	1.1	1,095	1.3
Total sectors	672,016.66	100	87,150	100

* Note: the technological centers[4] are included in the business sector.
Source: Own creation, using data from INE.

Technological Institute (ICT) was created as a nonprofit organization and promoted by the University of Navarre to facilitate contracts and provide service to companies. The University of Navarre's R&D services are commercialized by the ICT[5] through three research centers: CIFA (Center of Applied Chemistry Research), IBA (Applied Biology Institute), and CINDEB (Biomedical R&D Center); and two trademarks: EUROVIEW (formed by the audiovisual section of the Department of Computer Science) and CADIA (which commercializes research by the High Technical School of Architecture, with support from the Construction Center).

A recent study shows that one of the aspects to emphasize in Navarre's system is the great implantation of the University of Navarre. This relevance is basically due to the research conducted in medicine by the university's medical faculty, the University Clinic, and more generally, by the ICT. This combination is fast making the university into Navarre's second leading promoter agent for research, after private companies (Lavía, Olazarán, and Urrutia, 1995).

Lesson eighteen

BIBLIOGRAPHY

Gobierno de Navarra. 1999. Technological Plan of Navarra 2000–2003.

———. http://www.cfnavarra.es.

INE. http://www.ine.es.

Lavía, C, M. Olazarán, and V. Urrutia. 1995. *Los sistemas de ciencia y tecnología de la Comunidad Autónoma Vasca y Navarra: una visión desde los recursos económicos dedicados a proyectos de investigación.* Eusko Ikaskuntza.

Public University of Navarre. http://www.unavarra.es.

SODENA. 1990. Navarra, the Best Choice.

———. 1998. Navarra, Shall Be the Wonder of the World?

University of Navarre. http://www.unav.es.

Zabala, J. M. 1996. "La industria navarra frente al reto de la innovación: las actuaciones relativas a las PYMEs." *Economía Industrial* no. 312, pp. 167–176.

LEARNING GOALS

1. Document the evolution and main characteristics of the industrial sector in the FCN since the beginning

of the industrialization process in the 1960s. Stress the level of specialization, size of the businesses, and presence of foreign-owned companies.
2. Describe the role of the public sector in the industrialization process, including the aims of the principal measures implemented by the regional administration, especially through the current technology plan.
3. Discuss the main agents behind research and development expenses.

WRITTEN LESSON FOR SUBMISSION
1. Give your opinion about the links between the most important measures in the Technology Plan for 2000–2003 and the major industrial sectors of Navarre.
2. Search the website of the government of Navarre and explain the method of organization for controlling and evaluating the plan. To what extent do the different social and economic agents participate in this organization?

19 · Relationships of innovation
The Basque Autonomous Community

THE BASQUE COUNTRY as a whole was underdeveloped in research and development at the end of the 1970s. Most companies undertook no activity whatsoever in this field. The situation has progressively changed, however—especially in the BAC and, more recently, the FCN—as a result of the policies developed and the current trends in international competition. The evolution in recent years is given in Table 19-1.

The evolution of R&D expenditure in the FCN shows a marked upsurge in the late 1980s, followed by stagnation and a slight decrease throughout the 1990s. In the case of the BAC, expenditure increased notably in the early 1980s, followed by only small increases thereafter. Although the current rate exceeds the Spanish average, it is much lower than in the EU.

An analysis of expenditure and the full-time personnel working in R&D by the different agents is provided next (see Table 19-2); then, the main elements of the policies in effect will be summarized.

The way that R&D expenditures and the full-time personnel are organized by the different agents varies greatly by territory. In the FCN, the university's role in R&D activities stands out—especially that of the private university. In Spain, institutions of higher education are also highly relevant, especially due to low business participation. In the BAC, companies play the leading role; but it must be remembered that technology centers, although largely financed by the government, are included within this group.

The technology centers were founded through the already existing small testing and service laboratories associated with industrial centers and training schools.

Table 19-1
Percentage of R&D expenditure out of total GDP

	BAC	Spain	EU
1987	0.81	0.64	-
1988	0.94	0.72	-
1989	1	0.75	-
1990	1.13	0.85	2
1991	1.16	0.87	1.96
1992	1.17	0.91	1.92
1993	1.15	0.91	1.97
1994	1.04	0.85	1.9
1995	1.17	0.85	1.84
1996	1.23	0.87	1.82
1997	1.23	0.82	1.8
1998	1.2	0.9	-

Source: Lavia, C., et al. (2000) "Ikerketa eta garapena (I+D) Euskadin." Eusko Jaurlaritza and SPRI.

These centers have become one of the main components of the BAC's R&D sector. In some cases, they arose within the university: CEIT was created from the Engineering School of Navarre in San Sebastian, LABEIN's origins were in the School of Engineering of Bilbao, and TEKNIKER was born in the Engineering School of Mondragón. But they have never had an institutionalized relationship with the university; the moment they were established, they severed any such connections (Regis, 1998).

Rivalry
At the end of the 1970s, research and development lagged behind in the Basque Country. Thanks to the policies developed, it currently is ahead of the Spanish average.
Engraving from Jim Harter: Men, A Pictorial Archive.

THE RELATIONSHIP BETWEEN SCIENCE AND TECHNOLOGY POLICIES

The University of the Basque Country (UPV-EHU) was established in 1968 as the University of Bilbao to provide the region with a publicly funded institution of higher education. The university, which changed its name to UPV-EHU in 1977, is considered the most important higher-education institution in the Basque Country. It provides education in humanities, science, and technology.

Table 19-2
R&D expenditure and full-time personnel, by main agents of innovation (%)

FCN (1996)	R&D expenditures	Personnel
Public administration	4	4.5
Higher education	40	60.5
Business	56	35
Total	100	100

BAC (1998)	R&D expenditures	Personnel
Public administration	2.9	26.4
Higher education	25.2	4
Business	72	69.4
Total	100	100

Spain (1998)	R&D expenditures	Personnel
Public administration	16.2	20.7
Higher education	30.5	42.2
Business	52.1	35.7
Total	100	100

Source: INE, SPRI, and government of FCN.

Stable relationships between academics and business are relatively recent in Spain. These were legislated for the first time in 1983, when the University Reform Law (URL) came into force. Through this law, university departments and academics (through their departments) are allowed to sign contracts with public and private organizations, or with other individuals, to perform scientific, technical, or artistic jobs (article 11, URL). Academics were therefore able to collaborate with private companies legally to perform services for them or engage in joint activity for the first time.

In 1989, as a consequence of this law, an industrial liaison office by the name of Office of Research Output Transfer (OTRI) was created. OTRI belongs to a network of offices promoted by the central state administration's National R&D Plan. Its main task is to manage contracts signed by the university's academics and businesses or other organizations, public and private.

An organization fulfilling the same function served for the past decade by OTRI has existed since 1979 (prior to URL's passage): a university-business foundation called Euskoiker. Euskoiker has tried to promote ties between UPV-EHU and companies. It is currently closely linked to the university's Engineering School.

In 1981, the science policy was born, characterized until 1996 by its support for basic research. In 1997, combining the two types of policies implemented by the Basque government, the Scientific and Technological Plan (PCT) was created; it was in effect until 2000. This plan[6] has marked a radical change in the government's technological policy, exhibiting a comprehensive vision of science and technology.

The current Science and Technology Plan (1997–2000) is oriented toward the business sector as a whole. Among its objectives is integration of the university into industrial research. With the same objective of approaching and transferring the technology originated at the university to companies in accordance with their needs, three university-business programs have been launched.

ACCORDING TO an empirical research project financed by the EU (Universities, Technology Transfer and Spin-off Activities, 1996–98), among those academics who have had contact with industry, such contact has been initiated from the business side about half the time (50.9%). On the other hand, this research shows that members of engineering and computer departments are the academics with the most advanced, active industrial contacts. However, it is also salient that in every department, the initiators of the relationship are the companies, not the academics.

The most common business activities in which academics are engaged, in order of importance, are:
1. Large-scale scientific projects (56.2%)
2. Research contracts (47.6%)
3. Extrauniversity teaching (40.9%)

At the same time, the limited importance of the activity of companies created as a consequence of research developed at the university (spin-off companies) is noteworthy; these account for only 3.2% of the total, sometimes operating only in the engineering and science departments—and, even there, in very low percentages.

THE MOST frequent causes for nonfluid university-business relationships tend to be business distrust of university research, lack of confidentiality, different working rhythms, conflict of interests, lack of a history of cooperation with the productive sector, different incentives (curriculum-based in the academic environment, price- or efficiency-based in the industrial liaison offices), and the university's relative youth.

Some obstacles to the innovation system are as follows:
1. The technology centers are obliged to get funds from business, so research not closely market-related may be postponed.
2. The public administration and many small companies not involved in research activities do not collaborate.

3. The main aim is to answer company needs in the short run, so basic research is sometimes undervalued.
4. The university is often seen merely as the more technical departments (engineering, physics, chemistry, medicine), with the social branches forgotten.
5. The university does not promote the areas that most interest companies.
6. When companies are mentioned, the public administration usually refers to managers and technical staff, not workers.
7. Relations between employers and worker trade unions are often not very fluid.

Lesson nineteen

BIBLIOGRAPHY

Basque Government. http://www.euskadi.net.
———. 1996. Science and Technology Plan 1997–2000: A Summary.
Cooke, P., M. Gómez, and G. Etxebarria. 1997. "Regional Innovation Systems: Institutional and Organisational Dimensions." *Research Policy* 26:475–491.
Edquist, C. 1997. *Systems of Innovation: Technologies, Institutions and Organisations.* London and Washington: Pinter.
REGIS. 1998. Regis Project: Regional Innovation Systems: Designing for the Future. Targeted Socioeconomic Research.
University of the Basque Country. http://www.ehu.es.
University of Mondragón. http://www.muni.es.

LEARNING GOALS
1. Outline the evolution of R&D expenditure in the Southern Basque Country over the past decade and the number of people involved in these activities.
2. Describe technology centers and universities in order to analyze the relationship between the science and technology policies and the main agents (universities and companies) that advance them.
3. Show some obstacles within the innovation system.

WRITTEN LESSON FOR SUBMISSION
Compare the level of R&D expenditure during the past decade with respect to GDP and the evolution of the personnel involved in these activities in your country with the figures for the BAC. Also compare the main agents involved in such activities.

20 · Cooperatives and the social economy
The Basque Autonomous Community

SOCIAL ECONOMY is characterized by the existence of cooperatives, associations, and companies with varied legal statutes but with common principles and objectives. These focus on the nature of service to members or their environment; autonomous management and the primacy of democratic decision-making processes, people, and work over capital; and a share of the benefits.

Cooperatives continue to be a point of reference in matters of social economy, especially in the BAC. Cooperatives best represent the group of productive units which, unlike capitalist and public companies, are managed democratically by their users and evaluate capital based on its social utility.

DEFINITION OF THE SOCIAL ECONOMY: SOCIAL ECONOMY AGENTS

Social economy can be considered the group of private companies (1) whose activities in the market are those of producing goods and services, providing finance or insurance; and (2) in which benefit share and decision making are not directly linked to the capital contribution of each member. Participation in decision making is equal for all members, regardless of capital contributed. The social economy also includes economic agents whose main function is to provide services that will not be sold exclusively to some households and whose financial sector is implemented through voluntary contributions of the families acting as consumers.

The sector of private, nonprofit institutions provides not-for-sale services for the advantage of families. These services are provided according to social criteria and are financed not through a price but through the

Table 20-1
Agents of the social economy

Institutional sector	Social economy organizations
Nonfinance companies (production of goods and services for sale)	Cooperatives (consumers, associated work, housing, education, health care, sea, transportation, farming, and so on) Labor stock companies Farming transformation guilds Nonfinance mercantile companies controlled by social economy agents
Credit institutions	Credit cooperatives (rural savings banks and popular and professional credit cooperatives) Credit departments of cooperatives Savings banks
Insurance providers	Insurance companies Insurance cooperatives Social provision associations
Private, nonprofit Institutions	Associations, foundations, livestock and farming fraternities, fishing associations, mutual help organizations, Red Cross, and so on

Table 20-2
Number of cooperatives, by type (2001)

	BAC Cooperatives	%	Araba Cooperatives	%
Total	1,280	100	233	100
Farming	90	7	35	15
Consumer	30	2.3	2	0.8
Credit	2	0.1	—	—
Services	60	4.6	7	3
Education	86	6.7	12	5.1
Associated work	848	66.2	129	55.3
Housing	127	9.9	43	18.4
Others	37	2.8	5	2.1

	Bizkaia Cooperatives	%	Gipuzkoa Cooperatives	%
Total	531	100	516	100
Farming	28	5.2	27	5.2
Consumer	16	3	12	2.3
Credit	—	—	2	0.3
Services	26	4.8	27	5.2
Education	41	7.7	33	6,3
Associated work	383	72.1	336	65.1
Housing	29	5.4	55	10.6
Others	8	1.5	24	4.6

Source: Department of Justice, Work, and Social Security, Basque Government.

Collaboration
One of the main characteristic of cooperatives is that decision making and a share in benefits is not linked to the capital contribution of each member. All share equally.
Illustration by Seymour Chwast.

---

association contributive payment to those institutions. As these businesses are engaged in economic production and comply with the requirements mentioned in this subsection, they must be included within the rubric of social economy.

THE SOCIAL ECONOMY IN THE BASQUE COUNTRY
The following sections deal with two of the organizations within the social economy not engaged in financial activities: associated work cooperatives and labor stock companies.

ASSOCIATED WORK COOPERATIVES

Without doubt, the protagonist within the social economy is the group of cooperatives within the Mondragón Cooperative Corporation (MCC). MCC includes not only nonfinancial businesses, but also credit institutions and insurance companies (Caja Laboral and Lagun-Aro). As the special case of MCC will be dealt with elsewhere (see chapter 21), the focus here is on the Basque cooperative movement as a whole.

According to the Register of Cooperatives of the Basque government's Department of Social Security and Work, there were 1,280 cooperatives in 2001, 66.2% of them associated work cooperatives. This type of cooperative is the most common throughout the three territories of the BAC. The greatest number of farming cooperatives exist in Araba, the territory with the fewest cooperatives; this is due to the sector's relevance to Araba's economy. Bizkaia, in contrast, accounts for the greatest number of associated work cooperatives, while housing cooperatives reach their highest level in Gipuzkoa.

COOPERATIVE MEMBERS numbered 82,416, with 54% of them residents of Gipuzkoa. The majority of cooperative members, especially in Bizkaia, belong to consumer cooperatives. Logically, the highest number of farming cooperative members are from Araba. Lastly, Gipuzkoa has a greater diversity of members from different types of cooperatives.

It is noteworthy that the greatest number of cooperatives are those related to associated work, although their individual membership numbers are not very high. It is in associated work cooperatives that the largest number of cooperatives and jobs are concentrated. The most recent cooperatives of this type, however, are being founded primarily in the service sector.

Table 20-3
Number of members, by type (2001)

	BAC Members	%	Araba Members	%
Total	82,416	100	6,288	100
Farming	9,725	11.8	2,209	35.1
Consumer	28,196	34.2	254	4
Credit	83*	0.1	0	0
Services	2,091	2.5	195	3.1
Education	21,280	25.8	1,077	17.1
Associated Work	17,944	21.8	1,675	26.6
Housing	2,846	3.5	865	13.8
Others	224	0.3	13	0.2

	Bizkaia Members	%	Gipuzkoa Members	%
Total	31,177	100	44,951	100
Farming	3,203	10.3	4,313	9.6
Consumer	10,999	35.3	16,943	37.7
Credit	0	0	83*	0.2
Services	523	1.7	1.4	3.1
Education	9,741	31.2	10,462	23.3
Associated Work	6,365	20.4	9,904	22
Housing	305	1	1,676	3.7
Others	41	0.1	170	0.4

* According to the data provided by the Confederation of Cooperatives of the Basque Country, the number is 8,524.

Source: Basque Statistics Yearbook 2001, EUSTAT (2002).

Table 20-4
Labor stock companies (2001)

	Total	Araba	Bizkaia	Gipuzkoa
Labor Stock Companies	1,192	116	585	491
Total membership	13,349	1,078	6,939	5,332
Worker members	12,385	988	6,471	4,926
Capitalist members	964	90	468	406
Social capital (million pesetas)*	16,168	1,888	6,689	7,591
Economic activities	1,192	116	585	491
Agriculture	11	2	7	2
Industry	527	48	234	245
Building	180	22	106	52
Services	474	44	238	192

* Data from 1998.
Source: Basque Statistics Yearbook 2001; EUSTAT (2002).

The small size of the majority of associated work cooperatives subjects them to the typical problems of SMCs: insufficient capacity for innovation, problems of commercialization and foreign-market penetration, training and management deficiencies, and financing problems. FINANCING PROBLEMS are the result not only of their small size but also of the very nature of cooperatives, which focus on the relationship between work and capital to the detriment of the latter. Acquiring external financing is therefore complicated, and shortage of personal assets combines with the poor saving power of cooperative members to limit their contributory payments. Thus, the cooperative's assets and ability for self-financing turn out to be insufficient.[7]

LABOR STOCK COMPANIES (LSCS)

LSCs are the result of the difficult processes of sector and company reorganization. These processes took place from 1979 onward, the result of both many declarations of financial hardship and a process of rationalization in the Basque Country.

LSCs did not possess their own statutory framework until 1986. Earlier, they were constituted within the same legal framework used for all stock companies, except for a few statutory limitations regarding property and its transfer. Subsequently, LSCs were legally established as corporations in which 51% of the social capital belongs to the workers; working members and capital members coexist, dividing the social capital in the form of specific nominative shares for each type of member; and no member may own more than 25% of the aforementioned capital.

THE SPECIAL conditions of these companies demand collective action in obtaining personal, financial, and technical assistance in order to survive. The Basque Association of Labor Stock Companies (ASLE) was formed on July 22, 1982; in 2001, it consisted of a total of 289 businesses.

In 2001, according to data from the Department of Justice, Work, and Social Security, there were 1,192 labor stock companies employing a total of 13,349 members.

The distribution of these businesses by territory exhibits a concentration in Bizkaia, where are located the majority of LSCs active in the tertiary sector. Gipuzkoa comes next, with the idiosyncrasy that the importance of its industrial LSCs is higher than those in its tertiary sector. Lastly, there are 116 LSCs in Araba, distributed throughout all sectors.

LASTLY, DESPITE the fact that the majority of the LSCs currently in operation (approximately 60%) arose as the result of the closure and reorganization of earlier companies, the LSCs that emerged in the 1990s were small businesses in sectors such as computer science, engineering, business services, technical assistance, and transportation.

Lesson twenty

BIBLIOGRAPHY

Barker, J.A. 1997. "The Mondragon Model: A New Pathway for the 21st Century." In *The Organization of the Future*, F. Hesselbein, M. Goldsmith, and R. Beckhard, eds. San Francisco: Jossey-Bass Publications.

Basque Government. 1996. *Social Economy and Social Participation: The Ways of the Basques*. Instituto de Derecho Cooperativo y Economía Social, UPV.

MacLeod, G. 1997. *From Mondragon to America: Experiments in Community Economic Development*. Sydney and Nova Scotia: University of Cape Breton Press.

Taylor, T. L. 1994. "The Rhetorical Construction of Efficiency: Restructuring and Industrial Democracy in Mondragon, Spain." *Sociological Forum* 9:459–489.

LEARNING GOALS

1. Conceptualize the variety of agents and entities within the social economy.
2. Outline the main characteristics of the associated work cooperatives and labor stock companies in the BAC, including their sectorial distribution and basic problems.

181 · Cooperatives and the social economy

WRITTEN LESSON FOR SUBMISSION

Compare and contrast the characteristics of the two types of organizations that are included in the social economy that are not financial (take their strength within the BAC into account).

21 · The Mondragón cooperative system
A case history

WITHOUT DOUBT, the most important example of the Basque Country's social economy is the Mondragón Cooperative Corporation (MCC). Besides being an undeniable protagonist in both the Basque and Spanish social economies, it is noteworthy in its position as the most important industrial group in the Basque Country. In 1998, MCC generated 6% of the BAC's industrial GDP, employed 7% of the industrial sector's active population, and accounted for 10% of all industrial exports.

HISTORICAL EVOLUTION OF THE MONDRAGÓN COOPERATIVE EXPERIENCE
The origin of the groups goes back to 1956. That year Ulgor, Mondragón's first worker cooperative, was founded by five scholars from the Professional School[8] and the priest José María Arizmendiarrieta.

During these initial years of the Mondragón cooperative experience, other worker cooperatives appeared, stimulated by Ulgor's success and Arizmendiarrieta's promotion of social and educational awareness.[9]

It was also during these first stages that Arizmendiarrieta perceived the need to create a credit cooperative that, being fully identified with the project, could provide them with financial assistance.

On one hand, it was rather difficult for the cooperatives to obtain financial resources to make the investments necessary to attract private investors; on the other, private banks were unwilling to extend credit to worker cooperatives. Anyhow, the cooperatives would have lost their independence if they had borrowed from

Table 21-1
Impact of MCC in the Basque Autonomous Community (1998)

	GDP (million pesetas)	Employment	Exports (million pesetas)
Total BAC			
Total	5,155.46	779.8	1,607.93
Industry	1,885.610*	235	1,483.461**
Total MCC			
Total	233.056	24.676	–
Industry	111.236	16.6	157.351
% of the total			
Total	4.5	3.2	9.8
Industry	5.9	7.1	10.6

* From which 262.842 million pesetas are not purely industrial as they correspond to the energy and water sector.
** Without energy products exports.

Source: MCC webpage.

private banks. Again a result of Arizmendiarrieta's extraordinary vision, Caja Laboral Popular was officially founded in 1959.[10]

CAJA LABORAL initially provided public assistance to members because cooperatives were not covered within the mainstream social security system. It was thus established in its statutes that Caja Laboral would provide the cooperative not only financial services but also technical (Enterprise Division) and social services (Social Provision Service).

CAJA LABORAL EUSKADIKO KUTXA

Initially established to provide financial, technical, and social services to cooperatives, currently Caja Laboral offers a complete range of financial services not only to the corporation's cooperatives but also to third-party customers.

In 1967, the Social Provision Service, now called Lagun-Aro, became an independent cooperative. Since 1985, it has been a private system unique in Spain, due not to its financial magnitude but to the high benefits that cooperators receive in comparison to those provided by the Spanish public social security system.

IN 1977, THE IKERLAN cooperative was created to conduct applied industrial research.[11] Through Ikerlan's efforts, the cooperatives acquired knowledge and access to new, more advanced technologies.

In 1961, the first industrial complex was created: Ularco (renamed Fagor in 1985). It was initially composed of Ulgor, Arrasate, and Copreci, and later joined by Fagelectro and Ederlan (industrial cooperatives created in the Alto Deba region around that time).[12] The foundation of this first cooperative group set a precedent and, after a few years, the majority of cooperatives joined to form similar groups.

In 1980, four commercial groups existed: Fagor, Goilan, Orbide, and Learko. Throughout the 1980s, other groups were also formed: Nervión, Urkide, Indarko, Eibarko, Debako, Urcoa, Ulma, Erein, Goikoa, and Mugalde.

IN 1982, THE MONDRAGÓN Cooperative Group was created with two areas: financing (into which Caja Laboral and Lagun-Aro were integrated) and business (industrial, services and food, and agricultural). MCC was formed in 1991, during the Third Mondragón Group Congress.

MONDRAGÓN COOPERATIVE CORPORATION'S CURRENT STRUCTURE

In 1992, MCC was organized into three wide groups: financial, distribution, and industrial. The financial group is composed of the banking business, social provision, and insurance and leasing. The industrial group is made up of seven divisions devoted to industrial production. The distribution group includes the commercial distribution business and food activity. Among the training centers are the recently created University of Mondragón (1997), Mondragon Eskola Politeknikoa (specializing in engineering studies), Irakasle Eskola (Teachers' University School), and ETEO (business studies). Lastly, the research centers include Ikerlan, Ideko (a machine-tool sectorial center), and the Maier Technology Center (specializing in thermoplastics R&D).

THE FINANCIAL GROUP

The financial group includes the banking activities of Caja Laboral and the activities of Lagun-Aro, the social welfare organization of the MCC cooperatives. Caja Laboral offers a complete range of financial services to both the corporation's cooperatives and third-party customers. Lagun-Aro manages the corporation's own social security system, directing its financial activities towards optimizing returns. The activity of the group in the fields of insurance, leasing, and other types of parafinancial products is also noteworthy. In 1999, Lagun-Aro equity funds totalled 33.34 billion pesetas, while the resources administered by Caja Laboral amounted to 1,058.922 billion pesetas.

THE INDUSTRIAL GROUP

The industrial group is made up of 92 production companies, organized by sector into seven divisions. These divisions were created based on product-market homogeneity, regardless of prior local groups. Each division has as its foundation cooperative associations, all of which have a similar development strategy.

ACCORDING TO provisional 1999 data, the industrial group's sales reached 434.649 million pesetas, half of it in international markets. In 1998, the industrial group had seventeen production units in foreign countries and plans for significant future expansion, mainly in the Mercosur area (the common market made up of Argentina, Brazil, Paraguay, and Uruguay).

THE DISTRIBUTION GROUP

The distribution group includes the Eroski Cooperative (including Consum), which is the leading food-retailing company in Spain. In 1999, this group made 594.663 million pesetas in sales. Eroski and Consum's chain of stores in Spain consists of hypermarkets operating under the Eroski and Maxi logo, as well as Consum supermarkets and self-service stores. The company also

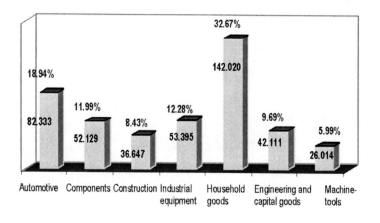

Figure 21-1.
Industrial group sales, 1999 (million pesetas); total sales: 434.649 million pesetas.

operates a chain of franchise outlets. Other business activities include a chain of travel agencies (Agencia de Viajes Eroski) and gas stations. This cooperative group also has its own laboratory, the backbone of its quality assurance program, to inspect the food it sells. The distribution group also includes the Erkop food subgroup, with activities like stockbreeding, horticulture, and food services.

THE MONDRAGÓN COOPERATIVE CORPORATION, AT PRESENT

As already noted, MCC is one of the most important groups in the Basque Country. In 1999, it generated 46,835 jobs: 46.23% were in the industrial group; 48.16%, in the distribution group; and 4.39%, in the financial group.

Industrial group
22,558

Distribution group
21,653

Financial group
2,059

Corporation activities
565

MCC made 889.76 million pesetas (5.348 million euros) of total sales in 1998; 238.647 million pesetas, or 26.8%, were in international markets. In 1998, MCC profits totalled 68.907 million pesetas (414 million euros), 31.8% higher than the previous year, and it made 70.763 million pesetas in investments.

Lesson twenty-one

BIBLIOGRAPHY

Mondragón Corporación Cooperativa. http://www.mcc.es.

Hacker, S. L. 1988. "Gender and Technology at the Mondragon System of Producer Cooperatives." *Economic and Industrial Democracy* 9:225–243.

Sperry, C. W. 1985. "What Makes Mondragon Work?" *Review of Social Economy* 43:345–356.

Whyte, W. F. 1995. "Learning from the Mondragon Cooperative Experience." *Studies in Comparative International Development* 30:58–67.

189 · The Mondragón cooperative system

LEARNING GOALS
1. Demonstrate the importance of the Mondragón Cooperative Corporation to the Basque economy.
2. Depict the evolution of the Mondragón cooperative system since its origin, including its current structure.

WRITTEN LESSON FOR SUBMISSION
Since the creation of the Mondragón group in the 1960s, this cooperative system has reached its present status through a lengthy evolution. Explain the different steps in this evolution and list the main characteristics of each phase.

22 · Social welfare coverage
Southern Basque Country

THIS CHAPTER begins by looking at different models of social welfare coverage. European and United States models differ in that in the former institutions play a fundamental role while in the latter it is largely a private affair. Next, after a brief overview of EU laws on social welfare coverage, the Spanish system of social welfare coverage will be examined. Then, the current jurisdictional powers of the Southern Basque Country in social welfare and the features of it that have been more fully developed in the Southern Basque Country will be presented. Such development has been conditioned, however, by the radical limitations of the current constitutional and statutory framework, counteracting Basque efforts to implement their own policy. The limitation of jurisdictional powers is a reflection of the strategic place that socio-labor matters currently have for the states, because of their importance to the state as a way of appearing to guarantee some welfare standards. Lastly, there is a reference to general aspects about social expenditure and its financing.

THE SPANISH SOCIAL SECURITY SYSTEM IN THE EUROPEAN FRAMEWORK
Generally speaking, there are three systems of social welfare coverage:
1. The model of countries such as the United States, Canada, or Australia, where the system of protection is primarily private in both its financing and in the benefits received through employer contributions and the employee payments.
2. The second model is widespread in northern European countries. This model has a universalist tradi-

tion in which everyone in need is covered. It is financed through income tax, and the benefits are considered inherent in the very status of citizenship, regardless of individual occupation or income level.
3. The third model is the one predominant in central and southern Europe (and thus in the Basque Country). It establishes public social security, specially financed through the social contributory payments of employers and employees. Benefits depend on the contributive payments made. The welfare system therefore depends upon salaried workers, and both its funding and provision reproduce the labor and social structure of each country. Jurisdictional transfer and services for the unemployed depend on the level of urgency and necessity, determined by the criteria established by each administration.

With regard to EU regulations over social welfare, the development of a policy for the entire union is not considered a priority.

THE EFFORTS OF the EU are dependent on the operations of the single market. In the same way that the EU tries to eliminate barriers to the free circulation of capital, goods, and services, it also aims at suppressing obstacles for the mobility and free circulation of workers. In matters of social policy, therefore, the only attempt to date has been directed at somehow countering the destabilizing effects of the emergence of a single European market, restricting EU legislative efforts aimed at protecting emigrants and guaranteeing gender equality.

Despite great differences in organization and financing methods, the social welfare systems of EU member states all share the objective of protecting people in situations of need, whether temporary (unemployment or

Soft landing
Social security has softened industrial reorganization, which hit particularly hard in the Basque Country in the 1980s. The combination of unemployment benefits and early retirement has facilitated the relatively "painless" removal of hundreds of thousands of employees from the job.
Watercolor by Ingo Fast.

childbirth) or permanent (retirement), regardless of their payment capacity.

In the Spanish state, social welfare falls under the public system of social security. The Spanish social security system is organized into different levels of protection. The highest tier corresponds to the "contributory" segment, which provides income that replaces that stemming from professional activity (as employee or self-employed), provided that the worker has already contributed to the social security system. The basic element of contributory benefits lies in pensions (retirement, widowhood, permanent disability, orphanhood), followed by unemployment benefits and temporary disability.

THE SECOND TIER is the "noncontributory" segment, designed to compensate people in situations of poverty because of lack of income; these people do not have to fulfill the condition of previous payment into the system because they cannot be ascribed to a specific professional group. Noncontributory benefits are, therefore, an important step towards universalization of social welfare coverage. Nevertheless, this level is very limited in Spain and appeared late, since it was created only in 1990. It covers only people who are disabled or older than sixty-five, without income, and have never participated in the contributory system (often because they did not work long enough to qualify for benefits).

Closely related to the already mentioned universalization and extension of protection to the impoverished segment of the population are public subsidies, whose development depends on the autonomous communities. Such subsidies are another part of coverage and are complementary to social security in several ways:

1. From a subjective point of view, by protecting people not covered by social security, because they are either

beyond its scope or, more frequently, have not made sufficient contributions. In recent decades, the requirements for qualifying for benefits have become more stringent. As a result, along with the volatility of the job market, there is an "expelling" effect from social security to not only the noncontributory levels but also public subsidies.

2. From an objective point of view, by extending benefits beyond the scope of social security, especially those related to widespread and long-term unemployment. The current regulation of unemployment benefits excludes a large segment of the population by demanding previous contributory payments from them and by reducing the benefits over a fixed period of time. In order to compensate, a number of European countries, among them the Southern Basque Country, have created the so-called minimum income insertion or social salaries.

3. Thirdly, social security benefits may not be sufficient, and they are supplemented by public subsidies because either they are running out of time, the amount of money does not cover emergency situations, or the benefits do not cover individual situations of poverty.

The last tier of social welfare coverage is private. Every citizen is entitled to obtain it, voluntarily and as a complement to public protection. This complementary level of social welfare coverage comprises a heterogeneous group of institutions, including savings plans and pension funds, voluntary improvements within collective business agreements, and mechanisms managed by companies.

Despite its private nature, however, intense public regulation has made it less independent from public provision. This is especially true in the case of collective entities, such as the Entidades de Prevision Social Voluntaria (EPSV, Organizations for Voluntary Social Provision), which are the most widely developed institutions in the Southern Basque Country, and over which the territories therein have exclusive jurisdictions.

THE BASQUE FRAMEWORK OF SOCIAL WELFARE COVERAGE

The Spanish Constitution prohibits a Basque social security system and establishes the basic legislation and economic system of social security as the exclusive jurisdiction of the state. The management of the economic system of social security would correspond to the Southern Basque Country, but the successive Spanish governments to date have prohibited its economic transfer. As a result, twenty years after the signing of the BAC's Statute of Autonomy and the FCN's Ley de Amejoramiento, all funds contributed to social security are still managed by state institutions.

SOME OTHER jurisdictional powers, however, have been transferred, including those regarding social security benefits related to social services (training and rehabilitation of the disabled and assistance to the elderly) and the administration of noncontributory benefits for retirement and disability. The contrasting postures of the Spanish government, which accepts the transfer of control over these benefits but rejects that over contributory benefits, is due to the latter's incomparably greater magnitude, which brings with it greater social legitimacy.

As already noted, public subsidies fall under the exclusive jurisdiction of the BAC and FCN. The laws of insertion income have been developed on that basis. In this respect, the Southern Basque Country has been a leader within Spain in the normative development of minimum insertion income, enforced since 1988 under the term *minimum insertion income* (IMI). Currently, the Southern Basque Country has the lowest poverty rate in the state, and the rate of poverty-stricken homes receiving benefits is also the highest (74%). As a whole, this affects workers in precarious situations who enter the job market intermittently and unstably.

In this respect, the Popular Legislative Initiative (ILP), presented in the Southern Basque Country in 1998 and discussed in the BAC's Parliament, merits attention. The minimum insertion income (also called basic income) proposed in the ILP significantly exceeds the limits of the current IMI in both amount (to be increased to meet the minimum wage) and coverage (extended to all individuals over 18, from a current minimum age of 25).

Lastly, with respect to private social welfare coverage, among those institutions that cover that complementary level of benefits, the Organizations for Voluntary Social Provision (which, as already noted, fall under the exclusive jurisdiction of the governments of the Southern Basque Country) are the ones that play the most relevant role in the Southern Basque Country. A good example is that the Basque Lagun-Aro, with assets of more than 250 billion pesetas, is the leading social provision association in the entire state. Furthermore, five Basque companies are ranked among the top ten in the state.

IN CONCLUSION, the aspects of social welfare in which the autonomous jurisdictional powers are more important are the two extremes: social services and insertion income on one hand, and private coverage managed by the EPSVs on the other.

Time off
Currently, the Southern Basque Country has the lowest poverty rate in the state, and the rate of poverty-stricken homes receiving benefits is also the highest (74%). People in need are helped, both the well-liked and the unloved.
Engraving from Harold Hart: The Illustrator's Handbook.

SOCIAL SPENDING IN THE BASQUE COUNTRY
Spending on social welfare has increased greatly in recent decades in the Southern Basque Country. The basic factors that explain this significant increase are the following:
1. The tremendous increase in social security economic benefits as a consequence of the growth of salaries

during the last twenty-five years; they are correlated through their contribution base although, as has been shown, the contribution of both net and gross salaries to the national income has decreased relative to business profits.
2. The increase in unemployment benefits due to the steep unemployment rate.
3. The demographic changes brought about by longer life expectancy; these affect not only retirement pensions (since they are going to be received over a longer period of time), but also health care and social services.

The rise in expenditure on social welfare is not the only result of the improvement of social welfare. Social security has softened industrial reorganization, which hit particularly hard in the Basque Country in the 1980s. The combination of unemployment and early retirement has therefore facilitated the relatively "painless" removal of hundreds of thousands of employees from the job.

SINCE 1994, IN both the Spanish state and the Southern Basque Country, social expenditure not only has not increased, it has declined. The trend of approaching the EU median has halted, with a five-percentage-point difference being sustained. Difference in both social expenditure compared to the GDP and the structure of expenditure are significant. The Southern Basque Country spends above the EU average on old age (although at a lower rate of GDP than the European average), unemployment, and social exclusion. Expenditure in all other spheres is also lower—especially family, basic necessities, and housing.

SOCIAL WELFARE FUNDING IN THE SOUTHERN BASQUE COUNTRY

The income structure for the funding of social welfare in the Southern Basque Country is very similar to that in central and southern EU countries. Over two-thirds of the resources come from social security contribution payments and the rest, nearly in its entirety, from public subsidies.

IT MUST BE emphasized that the structure and regulation of neither income nor expenditure can possibly be modified in the current statutory-constitutional framework. In this respect, there are no relative possibilities for independent regulation like those existing in the domain of taxes. Substate jurisdiction therefore cannot hope to do more than better administrate within the regulations imposed.

Lesson twenty-two

BIBLIOGRAPHY
Consejo Económico y Social. http://www.ces.es.
Instituto Nacional de Estadística. http://www.ine.es.
Ministerio de Trabajo y Asuntos Sociales.
    http://www.mtas.es.

LEARNING GOALS
1. Outline the different systems of social welfare coverage formulated in the most developed countries of the world.
2. Describe the characteristics of the current Spanish model.
3. Explain the specificities of the measures developed in the Southern Basque Country.

4. Delineate the jurisdictional allocation in social welfare coverage between the central state and Southern Basque Country and the evolution of social spending within the latter.

WRITTEN LESSON FOR SUBMISSION
1. Taking the different social welfare models developed in Europe into account, explain the areas in which the European Union intervenes.
2. Compare the system currently used in your country with the one developed in the Southern Basque Country.
3. In your opinion, what are the main reasons that the Spanish state refuses to transfer control of the social welfare system to the Basque Country in spite of the statutory agreement?

23 · The financial sector
Southern Basque Country

THE FINANCIAL sector is composed of a number of institutions, assets, and markets whose function is to channel the savings of economic units with a surplus towards those with a deficit and in need of funding. The main function of the financial sector is therefore to ensure that the economic system has the financial resources required in terms of volume, deadlines, costs, and so on.

In any economy, such units can be classified as the public administrations, nonfinance companies, finance companies (credit institutions and insurance companies), families, and the rest of the world. Currently, in the Basque Country, as in its neighbors, the public administrations and all its nonfinancing and financing companies function at a deficit—they receive net financing from the rest of the economy, while the families and the rest of the world present a credit balance.

COMPOSITION OF THE FINANCIAL SECTOR: CREDIT COMPANIES AND THE STOCK MARKET

Historically, mediation between savings units and those demanding funds has basically been carried out through credit companies (banks, savings banks, and credit cooperatives), although there have been significant changes throughout the world recently. These changes are resulting in a readjustment of the roles of the different financial mediators: credit companies do nonbanking business (insurance, investment funds), new financial mediators appear, and so on.

The intensive liberalization of the financial sector throughout the Spanish state bears no resemblance to that of the mid-1970s, when interventionist policies and

Transfer role
The financial sector is made of institutions, assets, and markets that channel a surplus towards those with a deficit and in need of funding.
Illustration by Seymour Chwast.

---

rigid regulations controlled the financing sector. As a result of Spain's entry into the EU, the process of reform was accelerated to meet the specifications for the creation of a single financial sector, thereby enabling the free circulation of capital and complete installation and provision of services throughout euro territory.

The 1998 foundation of the European Central Bank as the single monetary authority, with capacity to decide monetary policy for all the member states within euro territory, has meant a loss of member state sovereignty in financial matters. The present period is therefore one of transition, to consolidate a jointly coordinated functioning of the member states. Article 105 of the Maastricht Treaty establishes that the European Union's basic objective of monetary policy will be to maintain price stability (the Governing Council of the European Central Bank established this objective at an annual increase in prices below 2%).

CREDIT COMPANIES IN THE BASQUE COUNTRY
Credit companies include three groups of institutions, which are, in order of importance, banks, savings banks, and credit cooperatives. The three differ only in their legal component, since their financial activity in itself is legally equivalent.

FIVE BANKS have their headquarters in one or another of the four capitals of the Southern Basque Country: Banco de Bilbao Vizcaya Argentaria (BBVA), in Bilbao; Bankoa and Banco Guipuzcoano, in San Sebastian; Banco Vitoria (belonging to the group BSCH), in Vitoria-Gasteiz; and Banco Vasconia (within the group of Banco Popular), in Pamplona. (Not one bank, however, has its headquarters in the Northern Basque Country.)

In Spain, banks are organized as stock companies. They have all been private since 1998, following the final phase of privatization of Argentaria (the state-based public banking group). As a result of a plethora of mergers since the late 1980s, Spain's banking sector, although containing more than 150 companies, is organized into two large banking groups: the just-mentioned Banco de Bilbao Vizcaya Argentaria (BBVA), which has its headquarters in the Basque Country, and Banco Santander Central Hispano (BSCH).

The nature of the relationships between banks and nonfinancial businesses varies depending on the country. It is more distant in the United States and Great Britain and closer in countries such as Japan or Germany. In the Southern Basque Country, as throughout the state, such relationships have passed through different stages. Until 1975, credit companies were traditionally involved in business activities. During the industrial crisis, however, their investments declined; it was not until the mid-1990s that credit institutions again increased their participation in nonfinancial businesses—especially those related to strategic activities and expanding sectors. This change is intertwined with the process of privatization of public companies, some of them profitable, and the sharp increase in business benefits in recent years.

Savings banks constitute the second most active group of companies within the credit sector. Since their origins, savings banks have had a legal structure similar to that of foundations. In this sense, it must be mentioned that the law establishes that a minimum 50% of benefits be accumulated as reserves, while the rest should be used for social work in the territory in which the savings bank operates.

THE SAVINGS BANKS in the Southern Basque Country are Bilbao Bizkaia Kutxa (BBK), with its headquarters in Bilbao; Gipuzkoa-Donostia Kutxa (Kutxa), in San Sebastian; Vital Kutxa, in Vitoria-Gasteiz; and Caja de Ahorros de Navarra (CAN), in Pamplona. This last company arose from the merger (in effect since January 2000) between Navarre's two savings banks: Caja de Ahorros de Navarra and Caja Municipal de Pamplona.

Among the Basque Savings Banks, BBK and Kutxa are the most important.

The governments of the autonomous communities have broad jurisdiction over savings banks, from granting the license for their creation, fusion, or dissolution to control of credit and management activities, including inspection and penalization. A characteristic feature of savings banks, the result of both their historical origins and the legislation itself, is their bond to their native territory. The government of the BAC has repeatedly expressed its intention to consolidate its three savings banks, but clear steps in this direction have yet to be taken. On the contrary, for political reasons, the project is on hold.

IN REGARD TO their financial activities, since 1977, savings banks have been able to perform the same operations as banks. As a result of their historical evolution, however, their activity has been directed mainly to private individuals, small and midsize companies, and local institutions. On the other hand, the activity of savings banks in the mortgage market is noteworthy.

Credit cooperatives have the dual status of being both cooperative associations and credit companies. The autonomous governments of the Southern Basque Country are entitled to regulate their nature and legal framework.

One salient feature of these companies is that they must allocate 50% of their benefits for a promotion and education fund and 20% to obligatory reserves. Nonetheless, the operative capacity of credit companies is on a par with that of private banks and savings banks, except for the requirement that their members' financial needs must be met first.

The Southern Basque Country has the leading credit cooperative in the whole of the Spanish state: Caja Laboral (Euskadiko Kutxa), the financing company of the Mondragón Cooperative Corporation (MCC). The other two credit cooperatives in the Southern Basque Country are Caja Rural Vasca and Caja Rural Navarra, both of whose priorities lie in providing services to the timber, farming, and livestock-breeding sectors.

Currently, Caja Laboral continues its plan of expansion designed in the middle 1990s, which pursues an increase in new branch offices in the territories bordering the Southern Basque Country. Also noteworthy is its contribution to MCC's research and development programs, which amounted to 4.3 billion pesetas in 1999.

THE RECENT EVOLUTION OF CREDIT COMPANIES
An overview of the evolution of credit companies during the past two decades shows an increase in the relative importance of savings banks and credit cooperatives, at the expense of banks. Savings banks have grown more quickly than banks both in attracting savings and in granting credit, thereby increasing market participation share.

THE RECENT evolution of credit companies is related to the more pervasive economic progress of the second half of the 1990s, when GDP growth in the Southern Basque Country was slightly over the state average.

The good performance of these macroeconomic parameters is evident in the upsurge in the main indicators of activity of credit companies: sustained growth of deposit volume, outstanding expansion of credit, and increase in number of branch offices.

Each group's share of the credit market has stayed stable in recent years. On a state level, banks occupy the dominant position (53.7% of total credit in 1998), with savings banks second (41.5%) and credit cooperatives third (4.8%). In the Southern Basque Country, although

Double duty
Credit cooperatives have a dual status: they are both cooperative associations and credit companies. They are regulated by the autonomous governments of the Southern Basque Country.
Illustration by Jens Bonnke.

---

this order is the same, the percentages vary significantly. Banks and savings banks are less important than in the state (47.1% and 38.6%, respectively). This is due to the relative importance of credit cooperatives, which makes their share in the credit market ten points higher than in the state as a whole (14.3%). The majority of credit is usually granted in the BAC (81.6% in 1998), although the growth experienced by the FCN during the 1990s is noteworthy.

THE STOCK MARKET

To finance their investments, businesses with anonymous capital look for savings through the purchase of both stocks and bonds. The state itself resorts to public loans. The stock markets must therefore have the technical capacity to attract buyers and sellers daily, ensure the share prices of thousands of securities, and facilitate transactions according to officially fixed prices.

The Southern Basque Country is the site of the Stock Exchange of Bilbao, one of Spain's four stock markets. Of the trading in the state, 65% takes place in the Stock Exchange in Madrid, 20% in Barcelona, 10% in Bilbao, and 5% in Valencia.

Despite a weight relatively equivalent to those in other western European countries (such as Germany and France), the Spanish stock exchange is clearly less significant than those in the United States, Great Britain, and Japan. As a result, its contribution as a market for businesses to obtain investment funds is relatively low (only one-fifth of the 500 largest Spanish companies are listed on the stock exchange). Furthermore, the majority of trading involves a limited number of securities (especially financial companies, Telefónica, Repsol, and electric companies).

IN ADDITION, since the mid-1980s, the low volume and narrowness of the Spanish stock exchange has made it very dependant on foreign investors, whose objective is profit maximization. That dependence and its speculative nature combine to create a greater volatility of investment and, consequently, share prices.

Given the international nature of financial activities, the present and future of the Bilbao Stock Exchange depend largely on the widespread tendencies that mark technological progress (which delocalizes stock trading) and the evolution of the European Monetary Union. As the recent fusion of the London and Frankfurt Stock Exchanges demonstrates, the centralization of stock trading is generally accepted as a fait accompli.

In this context, the benefit of the Madrid Stock Exchange to the detriment of those others in the state is a real possibility. Specialization is the key for ensuring the survival of smaller exchanges such as Bilbao's. In the Bilbao Stock Exchange, the development of a variable income market for small and midsize companies is being pursued.

Nonetheless, as is true of stock markets as a whole, the Bilbao Stock Exchange was very dynamic throughout the 1990s, especially the second half of the decade. One example is that the 1999 revaluation rate was thirty times that of 1990.

This dynamism has occurred in a context of lowering interest rates (until November 1999), which has encouraged a large amount of family savings, bringing this into the variable income figures. The increase in internal consumption, which has invigorated home production and encouraged companies to be listed on the stock exchange, also merits mention.

Lesson twenty-three

BIBLIOGRAPHY
Banco Bilbao Vizcaya. http://www.bbv.es.
Bilbao Bizkaia Kutxa. http://www.bbk.es.
Bolsa de Bilbao. http://www.bolsabilbao.es.
Caja de Ahorros de Navarra. http://www.can.es.

LEARNING GOALS
1. Describe the composition and main functions of the financial sector.

2. Show the characteristics and recent evolution of the main credit companies and the stock market located in the Basque Country.

WRITTEN LESSON FOR SUBMISSION
1. Describe the main features of each of the groups of institutions that are considered credit companies and evaluate their share in the credit market of the Basque Country.
2. List the main functions of the stock exchange and describe the evolution of the Bilbao Stock Exchange within the Spanish market.

24 · Current economic indicators

SINCE THE mid-1980s, the Basque economy has enjoyed a period of sustainable growth, increasingly feeling the influence of European economies. The period from 1985 to 2000 was marked by recovery and growth, interrupted only by the short, but deep European crisis of the early 1990s.

The year 1985 thus marks the beginning of the Basque economy's recovery, stimulated not only by the adjustment policies implemented but also by the international economy's recovery and Spain's integration into the then-EEC.

The Basque economy is currently going through an excellent period, outperforming Spain's. The Basque Country's economic growth in 1998, for example, exceeded both Spain's (3.8%) and Europe's (2.8%). Recent years have thus represented one of the best periods of the past decade, especially for industrial activity and employment creation. In this chapter, the Basque economy's current characteristics—its production structure, the labor market's situation, and finally, per capita income levels—are discussed.

THE CURRENT BASQUE PRODUCTIVE STRUCTURE

As previously noted, with the exception of the sharp crisis of the early 1990s, the Basque economy has grown continuously in recent years. The BAC's production has increased annually, with the 1998 increase particularly noteworthy. The growth of the FCN's economy in the 1990s has also been great, even exceeding the BAC's.

One of the characteristics of the BAC's economic structure is that 50% of the GDP comes from Bizkaia, a territory in which the 1990s crisis had the greatest impact. On the other hand, although the BAC's service sector

Table 24-1.
Evolution of the GDP in market prices by historical territory (million pesetas)

	Value FCN	IPY*	Value Araba	IPY*
1998**	–	–	847.506	5.8
1997	1,321.44	6.1	800.669	5.9
1996	1,244.71	6.3	756.011	4.3
1995	1,170.48	9.4	724.596	3.9
1994	1,069.27	7.4	697.684	4.7
1993	995.248	–	666.151	0.4
1992	–	–	663.748	0.8
1991	935.765	–	658.483	5.5
	Bizkaia		**Gipuzkoa**	
1998**	2,572.43	5.1	1,669.92	5.2
1997	2,447.83	4	1,587.49	4.2
1996	2,354.16	2	1,523.90	2.2
1995	2,306.90	2.9	1,491.56	4.4
1994	2,242.90	2.7	1,428.41	3.6
1993	2,183.02	−1.8	1,378.23	0.3
1992	2,222.07	0.9	1,374.07	0.3
1991	2,202.51	2.2	1,369.99	1.2
	BAC			
1998**	5,089.855	5.2		
1997	4,835.99	4.4		
1996	4,634.07	2.5		
1995	4,523.06	3.5		
1994	4,368.99	3.3		
1993	4,227.40	−0.8		
1992	4,259.89	0.7		
1991	4,230.99	2.4		

* IPY = Increase over previous year (%)
** Provisional data

Source: EUSTAT, *Cuentas económicas*; Fundación BBV.

has grown considerably in recent years, industry's contribution to the GDP is 41%.

REGARDING THE FCN, according to recent data, its 1997 gross added value in agriculture was 57.266 million pesetas; in industry, 446.223 million pesetas; in construction, 82.75 million pesetas; and in the service sector, 667.828 million pesetas. On the other hand, 35.521 million pesetas of taxes were linked to produc-

Table 24-2
GDP distribution by sectorial activity in the BAC (million pesetas)

	1995	1996	1997	1998*
Agriculture	66.079	64.179	67.354	69.877
Industry	1,825.762	1,853.971	1,961.881	2,099.527
Industry (excl. construction)	1,517.418	1,548.407	1,650.495	1,769.749
Construction	308.344	305.564	311.386	329.778
Services	2,315.096	2,386.721	2,465.151	2,557.783
Trade, hotels, transportation	975.902	987.201	1,013.579	1,056.437
Bank, insurance, business services	689.318	736.026	777.327	813.221
Other services	649.876	663.494	674.245	688.125
Taxes linked imports	10.117	9.882	9.469	10.355
VAT	306.002	319.313	332.130	352.313
GDP market prices	4,523.056	4,634.066	4,835.985	5,089.855

* Provisional data
Source: EUSTAT, *Cuentas económicas*.

Right direction
The Basque economy is currently going through an excellent period, outperforming Spain's.
 One of the characteristics of the BAC's economic structure is that 50% of the GDP comes from Bizkaia, a territory in which the 1990s crisis had the greatest impact.
Illustration by Jennifer Thermes.

---

tion. Lastly, the FCN's total GDP in 1997 (the most recent year in which data was available) was 1,321.438 million pesetas.

BAC INDUSTRY currently exports 29% of the autonomous community's GDP to foreign countries. The BAC's export propensity[13] is the highest of all surrounding economies (above Germany's highly open

Table 24-3
Employment by sector (1998)

	BAC	%	FCN (2000)	%
Active-age population	955,900	100	231,000	100
Working population	849,400	88.8	217,000	94
Agriculture and fisheries	14,600	1.7	15,500	7
Industry	257,400	30.3	66,100	29
Construction	75,000	8.8	20,100	9
Services	502,400	59.2	115,800	50
Unemployed population	106,500	11.2	13,600	6

Source: Basque Statistics Yearbook 2001, EUSTAT (2002) for BAC, and INE for FCN.

economy, and much higher than Spain's). The automotive, machine-tool, smelt, iron, steel (including its derivative products), and rubber-product sectors account for 60% of exports, thus demonstrating the BAC's industrial concentration and specialization.

IN THE TERTIARY sector, which accounts for 50% of the BAC's production, the bank, insurance, and advanced services to business are prominent, accounting for 15.9% of the GDP.

Analyzing employment by sector, 59.4% of the BAC's population is employed in the service sector and 30.3% in industry. On the other hand, it is noteworthy that the FCN's unemployment rate is lower than that of the BAC, with industry accounting for 28.6% of FCN employment.

THE LABOR MARKET SITUATION
The past two decades, the situation of the labor market throughout Spain has been worrisome. This is especially

Table 24-4
Active and unemployment rates

	BAC Active rate	Unemployment
1985	51.0	21.1
1989	52.6	18.8
1990	51.9	16.2
1992	52.9	19.9
1994	52.5	25.0
1996	52.5	22.4
1999	53.9	15.5
2000	54.2	14.8
2001	53.4	11.1*

*A change in the methodology used to get the data was implemented in 2001, which breaks the comparableness of the data.
Source: Basque Statistics Yearbook 2001; EUSTAT (2002).

Table 24-5
Unemployment by gender (2001)

	BAC	
Unemployed population	106,500	11.1%
Male	42,800	40.2%
Female	63,700	59.8%

Source: Basque Statistics Yearbook 2001; EUSTAT (2002).

so in the BAC, where unemployment reached 23.9% in the mid-1980s (in 1986). More recently, the BAC's labor market has created employment at a rapid rate, mainly in the industrial sector.

As already noted, in the past decade, the number of working individuals has shattered all records (849,000); as shown in Table 24-3, in 2001, unemployment has decreased to 11.1% (at last approaching the rate of the early 1980s—see chapter 7).

Regarding the breakdown of unemployment, as shown in Table 24-5, the high rate of women is noteworthy.

INCOME PER CAPITA: CURRENT LEVEL INDICATORS
After the restructuring and adaptation processes of the past decade, and the periods of crisis and economic

Table 24-6
European region's economy, GDP per capita (1996)

	Population (thousands)	GDP in in ECUs	GDP per capita in ECUs	GDP per capita EU-15 =100
EUR-15	372,672.60	6,781,008	18,103	100
Spain	39,241.90	471,688	11,891	79
BAC	2,072.90	29,211	13,933	92
FCN	526	7,706	14,812	98
Madrid	5,012.50	76,273	15,190	101
Balearic Isl.	727.6	11,161	14,656	97
Catalonia	6,066.80	91,110	14,968	99

Source: Eurostat.

development experienced by the Basque economy, current per capita income levels are very positive.

The Basque Country, although still far below the average European GDP per capita, is nevertheless one of the richest regions of Spain, beneath only the autonomous communities of Madrid, Catalonia, the Balearic Islands, and Navarre, as seen in Table 24-6.

Lesson twenty-four

BIBLIOGRAPHY
EUSTAT. http://www.eustat.es.
Fundación BBV. http://www.bbva.es.
INE. http://www.ine.es.

LEARNING GOAL
Describe the current economic situation of the Southern Basque Country, taking its evolution during the past decade into account. Use the production structure, labor market, and per capita income levels as your main points of reference.

WRITTEN LESSON FOR SUBMISSION
Compare and contrast the current economic situation of the Basque Autonomous Community with that of the Foral Community of Navarre. Base your answer on the main indicators of their respective economies.

25 · Metropolitan areas, part I

NEW PROTAGONISM OF URBAN AREAS

The structural crisis of the mid-1970s and the resulting new international economic context have brought about significant changes worldwide. International economic globalization has combined with the development of new technologies to produce spatial reorganization, with new functions assigned to different territories.

1. Profound transformations are taking place in the productive structure. Traditional industries, until recently the very basis of the economy, have lost significant ground due to the difficulties of competing with the greater cost-efficiency of developing countries. New industries of high technology and advanced productive services have emerged as the fundamental tool for specialization in production. The most suitable conditions for those industries and activities are found in urban and metropolitan areas.
2. New technologies (especially telecommunications) provide new possibilities for the expansion of economic activity. On the other hand, management and control activities are based in the largest cities (the so-called global cities), because they possess social agents, infrastructures, and the necessary types of production.
3. In recent decades, financial markets, companies offering advanced services to businesses, big banks, and the headquarters of transnational companies have all tended to base themselves in large cities. Such cities and their surroundings have therefore become strategic locations for the functioning of a globalized economy.

THE BIG INTERNATIONAL METROPOLIS

Cities with a higher degree of internationalization present a series of characteristics related, on one hand, to their metropolitan nature and, on the other, to their international status.

Characteristics related to the condition of metropolis include the following:

1. In big metropolitan areas, besides numerous resources and prosperous business activity, there is an ample consumer market. Large urban populations also offer other advantages, such as availability of different types of infrastructure and basic equipment, numerous specialized high-quality services for both companies and individuals, a dense industrial productive framework that facilitates relationships among companies, and more highly structured social organization.
2. In big cities, there is great activity related to the tertiary sector, management, and organization.
3. In big cities, the job market is diversified and active. In the majority of such cities, a large number of unqualified workers coexist with a concentration of qualified workers. This is decisive for innovation, which requires both qualified professionals and low-qualified workers.

In addition, large metropolitan areas possess technological centers, colleges, and an environment that generally encourages the development of intellectual resources.

ALL THESE RESOURCES contribute to the spread and circulation of information and innovation, not only within metropolitan areas but also, through foreign networks, among them.

Rustbelt
Blast furnace of the Altos Hornos. Traditional industries, until recently the very basis of the economy, have lost significant ground due to the difficulties of competing with the greater cost-efficiency of developing countries.
Photo: Iñaki Uriarte

Characteristics related to a metropolis's international character include the following:

1. Transnational corporations have widened their networks of international subsidiary companies, promoting the development of relationships among those companies, known as intrafirm relationships. This internationalization process favors cities in which the central headquarters of corporations are established. The expansion of both financial flow and international markets of advanced services also contributes to the process of internationalization of the cities in which such financial and service markets are based.
2. In this context, without overlooking the importance of other infrastructural networks, the existence and development of telecommunication networks becomes absolutely necessary (albeit not sufficient) for ensuring the internationalization process.
3. The great mobility of the population is another characteristic of international cities. Despite the fact that there are different groups of citizens, the professional elites arising from economic and technological exchanges are the most relevant to both this mobility and the internationalization of cities. These "circulating elites" are continuously moving between cities to conduct their business. International cities must therefore meet the requirements for short stays (airports, business areas, international hotels), and at the same time offer adequate lodging for such elites.
4. International cities are connection and communication nodes within large infrastructural networks. The patterns that currently define communication networks emphasize that cities be adequately interconnected within those networks. The development of high-speed transportation (by air, road, or train) and telecommunications thus becomes particularly criti-

cal. International traffic therefore tends to concentrate within a few metropolitan areas, thus increasing their logistic advantages.

METROPOLITAN REVIVAL AS THE AXIS OF DEVELOPMENT POLICIES

As large metropolitan areas have been very successful in achieving high development rates, strategies and policies to promote the main town in an area and create the conditions for it to become an international metropolis have recently emerged. The main objective is therefore the international dimension, which does not necessarily benefit strategies for adapting the development of the town and its surroundings to the needs of the region and its inhabitants.

IN MOST CASES, local authorities (of the town or metropolis) undertake projects and implement policies with the participation and financial contribution of regional and state authorities.

Some of the aims of those policies are to:
1. Provide infrastructure that enables easy access into towns and lodgings, such as airports, ports, highways, high-speed trains, hotels, convention centers, and chambers of commerce.
2. Establish business centers and technological sites, so as to promote the foundation of advanced companies and encourage economic activity; as a complement to the latter, to promote the infrastructure necessary for university training and education and to support research and technological expansion.
3. Stimulate the development of a broad sector of advanced services. This will promote the development of high-technology facilities, create incentives for companies to establish themselves in the region, and make the city more attractive through the loca-

Global yardstick
International economic globalization has combined with the development of new technologies to produce spatial reorganization, with new functions assigned to different territories.
Watercolor by Robin Jareaux.

---

    tion of business headquarters and decision centers of transnational companies or international institutions (mainly European).
4. Devise international marketing initiatives, such as organizing significant sports and cultural events and creating special services and agencies to promote the

metropolis abroad. The aim of these events is to project the image of a modern, advanced, internationally well-connected city governed by efficient administrators.
5. Take actions to renew the city or create new centers within it, recovering building sites as the consequence of dismantling old industrial plants and outdated infrastructure ignored by the economic reorganization; since these urban centers are highly valued, they become sites for advanced business activity, skilled labor, and high-quality housing.

THE PREVIOUSLY mentioned strategies form the basis of most plans and urban renewal policies. As already noted, the objective is to improve a city's competitiveness on an international level. Nevertheless, programs such as social housing programs and programs against poverty and social exclusion are often implemented in order to counteract the negative consequences of such policies and thereby eliminate potential criticisms.

In closing this chapter, it is worth offering some reflections on such policies:
1. Large cities included in international networks will have great advantages over those cities and territories excluded. This is because investment and growth will be directed to cities well-connected and specialized in high-technology industries and services. In addition, spatial polarization will increase as a consequence of the development of communication and high-speed transportation infrastructures, because these are aimed at connecting large specialized centers. However, it will be common for a city's relationships with other cities to be reinforced, while those with its natural region are weakened; in other words, because of

these networks, the closer the relationships among big cities, the less intense the relationships between a city and its region.
2. On the other hand, the mere application of such policies does not imply that any city automatically becomes an advanced international metropolis.
a. The international urban hierarchy is, actually, rather rigid, and international functions are concentrated within a small number of privileged cities; in fact, this nucleus of decision is composed of cities that, as a result of their own evolution, became international metropolises and have been reinforced by the structural reorganization of recent times (for example, the increasing importance of new technologies in production processes and the primacy of the tertiary sector in advanced economies).
b. In big cities, concentration in dynamic sectors and activities is on the rise. Such activities, however—especially those of a high level—will only be possible in certain metropolitan areas. Technological capacity will be the determining factor in economic development and regional growth. On the metropolitan level, initiatives to encourage the characteristics of an innovative environment are absolutely essential and do not stop at the mere provision of infrastructure.
3. The social and spatial consequences of the development model, promoted by the strategies and policies already mentioned, must also be taken into account. Inequalities may emerge in the metropolis, for example, between those areas with higher investment and activity concentration and those that are excluded (towns and working-class districts that arose in the industrial era but currently suffer from social, environmental, and town-planning problems).

Moreover, inequalities may increase throughout the region, because the application of development policies, based in the leading urban areas, will have consequences for the region as a whole. If the public authorities concentrate their efforts and resources on metropolitan renewal without considering complementary or compensatory measures for the rest of the region, inequalities within the region are bound to increase.

4. Certain problems arising from the design and implementation of such projects may endanger the viability of the project itself. On one hand, the different administrative levels within a metropolitan area (town councils, metropolitan institutions, state administration, regional administration, other public organizations) have different jurisdictions; as a result, they frequently have discrepancies. On the other hand, the mechanisms to promote public participation are completely inefficient; the attempts at and means for polling civil society's opinions are also very limited. In any case, business organizations and institutions are given preference over popular initiatives. Solving these two problems may prove vital to ensuring a strategy that guarantees the future of town and region alike.

Lesson twenty-five

BIBLIOGRAPHY

Batten, D. F. 1995. "Network Cities: Creative Urban Agglomerations for the 21st Century." *Urban Studies* 32(2):313–327.

Bonneville, M. 1994. "Internationalization of Non-capital Cities in Europe: Aspects, Processes and Prospects." *European Planning Studies* 2(3):267–285.

Castells, M. 1989. *The Informational City—Information Technology, Economic Restructuring and the Urban-Regional Process.* Oxford: Blackwell.

Sassen, S. 1991. *The Global City: New York, London, Tokyo.* Princeton, NJ: Princeton University Press.

———. 1994. *Cities in a World Economy.* Thousand Oaks, CA: Pine Forge Press.

LEARNING GOAL

Document the role played by metropolitan areas in the international context as promoters of regional and local development.

WRITTEN LESSON FOR SUBMISSION

1. Describe the characteristics of the main metropolitan and urban areas of your country.
2. Do a case study of a metropolitan or urban area in your country, explaining the policies applied and their success with regard to local and regional development.

26 · Metropolitan Areas, part II
The urban system in the Basque Country

THE URBANIZATION process in the Basque Country was belated in comparison to that elsewhere in Europe. The beginnings of the process of development of Basque towns could be placed in the early middle ages, between the twelfth and fourteenth centuries. It arose for reasons that were military-political (kings' efforts to keep territory under their control) and commercial-economic (demographic growth, surplus of the farming workforce, the need to create stable markets).

The impact of various economic crises and plagues inhibited the significant growth of towns until fairly recently. As a result of the industrialization process that began in the nineteenth century and gradually consolidated, cities began to grow—at first slowly, and later (especially in the midtwentieth century) more rapidly.

Population growth has accelerated since the midtwentieth century because of industrial and economic development and a tendency toward concentration. This process has been more clearly evident in Araba and Navarre because their industrialization, demographic growth, and urban concentration had been slow since the nineteenth century. Although these processes had earlier (late-nineteenth century) beginnings in Bizkaia and Gipuzkoa, they were reinforced in these two territories as well during the 1960s. People moved to the cities in increasing numbers, especially the capitals (Bilbao and San Sebastian), because these were the industrial motors.

The evolution of the Northern Basque Country has been different. The growth of Bayonne has depended on the development of the district under its dominion. The city, with an ever increasing population, has become the

Table 26-1
Population concentration in major cities

Territory	Population	Capital	Population	% Capital /territory
Araba	286,177	Vitoria-Gasteiz	217,369	75.9
Bizkaia	1,139,012	Bilbao	356,045	31.2
Gipuzkoa	678,871	San Sebastian	179,336	26.4
Navarre	538,009	Pamplona	180,483	33.5
Northern Basque Country	262,311	Bayonne	40,113	15.3

Source: Own creation based on the data provided by EUSTAT (31-12-1998); Statistics Institute of the Government of Navarre (01-1-1999) and INSEE (1999).

main functional center of that district. In 1857, with a population of 35,000, Bayonne was the largest Basque city; at the moment, it has 42,000, putting it very low in the current ranking.

OVERVIEW OF THE BASQUE URBAN SYSTEM
Mirroring trends throughout Europe, the population density in the largest cities has increased over the past century.

THIS PROCESS of concentration is clearly observable in the significance of the capital cities, as shown in Table 26-1. Particularly noteworthy is the case of Vitoria-Gasteiz, which accounts for a macroconcentration of 76% of Araba's total population.

Bilbao must be discussed in terms of its entire metropolitan area (including the surrounding towns); greater

Bilbao has 887,521 inhabitants—77.75% of Bizkaia's total population.

In the Northern Basque Country, the concentration of population on the coast is also noteworthy. The urban conglomeration of Bayonne-Anglet-Biarritz (BAB) presently has 112,403 inhabitants, 42.8% of the Northern Basque Country's total, while 23.7% live on the rest of the coast, in Labourd.

THE SIZE OF the different towns thus shows the sharpest demographic imbalance in Araba, Bizkaia, and Labourd. Gipuzkoa and Navarre, in contrast, offer both greater distribution of population and more balanced urban systems. The situation of Basse Navarre and Soule is very different; most towns have under 500 occupants, and these numbers are on the decline.

URBAN HIERARCHY

In the current Basque urban hierarchy, the following tiers can be distinguished:
1. Greater Bilbao
2. San Sebastian, Vitoria-Gasteiz, Pamplona, and Bayonne
3. Eibar, Irun, Bermeo, Durango, Altsasu, Tudela, and Tolosa, among others
4. Elgoibar, Zarautz, Azpeitia, Azkoitia, Laudio, Amurrio, Balmaseda, Agurain, among others

The network of towns and villages could be completed in this manner. As can be observed, the cities on the first two tiers, especially Bilbao, would be the main points of reference of the Basque metropolitan model. The towns should not be forgotten, however, because they serve the essential function of providing territorial balance. This function can be reinforced or weakened, depending on the territorial model chosen and implemented.

RELATIONSHIPS AMONG TOWNS

In both the Northern and Southern Basque Country, the main economic relationships, administrative structures, financial relationships, means of transportation, and so on are configured by France and Spain, respectively. This singular fact accounts for the evolution of two distinct, highly differentiated urban systems.

The Northern Basque Country falls under the influence of two cities, Bayonne and Pau (Béarn). Labourd and Basse Navarre are oriented toward Bayonne, while Soule is oriented towards Pau. On the other hand, the towns in the Southern Basque Country fall under the influence of their territorial capitals; some areas on the periphery, however, such as southern Araba and the Ribera in Navarre, fall under the influence of Miranda de Ebro and Logroño.

The area of influence of Bilbao, however, spreads beyond the Basque territory, reaching into northern Burgos and eastern Cantabria. Moreover, Bilbao's transportation network is essential to the Basque urban system's integration into and connection with other European cities and their surroundings.

CHARACTERISTICS OF THE MAIN CITIES AND METROPOLITAN AREAS

With nearly a million inhabitants, greater Bilbao clearly ranks first, both within the Basque Country (for number of inhabitants and functions), and in its role within the Spanish state. Bilbao is by far the northern Iberian peninsula's largest and most important metropolitan area.

Economy and politics
The first Basque towns date back to the late Middle Ages, between the twelfth and fourteenth centuries. Kings needed to control territory. Their subjects needed stable markets.
Woodcut from the Nüremberg Chronicle, *1493*.

Greater Bilbao includes the capital and its surroundings: both sides of the Nervion River, the areas of Hego-Uribe and Txoriherri, and some neighboring towns.

Beginning in the late nineteenth century, Bilbao became industrial. The process of industrialization subsequently intensified and spread to the rest of the metropolitan area. As a result of the crisis of the 1970s, however, the town experienced difficulties. Sharp industrial decline and its aftermath (high unemployment, increase in social exclusion), environmental degradation, and the town planning model (due to savage industrial development) combined to create doubt about future perspectives.

In order to avoid a bleak future for Bilbao, however, local political, economic, and social leaders ushered in a new phase. Production will now be based on the promotion of the tertiary sector and the technological renewal of industry. The image, functioning, structure, and many other aspects of the entire metropolitan area will also be completely transformed.

Despite the fact that San Sebastian is the smallest capital in the Southern Basque Country, taken in conjunction with its surrounding towns (including Errenteria, Pasaia, Hernani, and Lasarte-Oria), it is the second leading metropolitan area.

THE GROWTH OF San Sebastian started during the second half of the nineteenth century, in the industrialization period. At the end of the Civil War, industrialization intensified. As a consequence, the population increased and the city grew quickly. The last quarter of the twentieth century also witnessed change; the economic crisis had a negative impact, and in the wake of the crisis some subsequent projects attempted to renew the city.

With respect to functions and services, great gaps exist between the city's center and its outlying areas. The capital serves administrative, political, cultural, and commercial functions. The outlying areas, in contrast, fulfill industrial and commercial functions; these are made up of bedroom towns for area workers and often suffer from a lack of services.

The creation of industrial districts by political authorities in the 1960s promoted industrial development in Vitoria-Gasteiz, leading it to evolve from a small commercial town into a service and industrial center.

ARABA'S ECONOMIC growth currently exceeds that of both the BAC and Spain. Vitoria-Gasteiz and its area have an important role in that growth, since 80% of the territory's population and the majority of economic activity are concentrated there. The area is also proving highly successful in attracting foreign investment and companies.

Two elements have contributed significantly to this positive evolution: the advantages reaped from the selection of Vitoria-Gasteiz as the BAC's administrative capital; and the availability of large sites for the development of economic activity.

As in other cities, administrative, commercial, and financial activities are conducted in the center, residential areas are located in its surroundings, and the industrial area is outside of the city.

Pamplona is the center of an urban network that is more balanced than those in the other territories. Its population increased during the first half of the twentieth century, as the people from Navarre's villages moved into town. The greatest growth, however, took place from the 1960s onwards, due to the intensification of the industrialization process. Such development resulted in the emergence of a metropolitan area around Pamplona, including Atarrabia, Burlata, and Uharte. The concentration of population in Pamplona and its metropolitan area may endanger the balance of the territory's urban system (it holds more than 50% of Navarre's current population). On the other hand, the administrative division between the FCN and the BAC has promoted the city's centralizing pull, since many towns and areas previously having relationships with other Basque territories now depend on Pamplona.

With respect to the importance of the productive sectors, the service sector is the leader in Pamplona, with mainly commercial and public services predominating (education, health, and administration) and a high concentration of services in the hospital field and university education. Industry is also significant, but it is located in the surrounding areas and towns.

IN THE NORTHERN Basque Country, Bayonne and its metropolitan area (the BAB conurbation formed with Anglet and Biarritz) is the largest urban conglomeration. It extends along the coast, from Gipuzkoa in the south to Les Landes in the north. The majority of commercial activity and public and professional services are concentrated in Bayonne and its surroundings. Most of the Northern Basque Country's industry is also located in the BAB conurbation.

The most significant feature of the Northern Basque Country is the great coast/inland divide: while demographic dynamism (owed largely to positive net migration) and economic activity are centered on the coast, the inland population is declining. In order to counter this trend, policies that restore a degree of balance and provide substantial subsidies will be necessary.

Lesson twenty-six

BIBLIOGRAPHY
Bilbao Metropoli 30. http://www.bm30.es.
Gómez Uranga, M. 1998. "Reflective Images: the Case of Urban Regeneration in Glasgow and Bilbao." *International Journal of Urban and Regional Research* 22.
———., and G. Etxebarria. 2000. "Panorama of the Basque Country and its Competence for Self-Government." *European Planning Studies* 8(4):521–535.

LEARNING GOAL
Describe the Basque urban system, showing its tendencies and determining its main urban areas.

WRITTEN LESSON FOR SUBMISSION
1. What elements contribute to economic activity and demographic concentration in the main Basque metropolitan areas?
2. Explain the fundamental differences among the main Basque urban areas. Are they complementary, or do they compete in their operations?

27 · The Northern Basque Country, part I[14]
Economic Framework

THE NORTHERN Basque Country, also known as Iparralde, consists of three territories: Labourd, which is on the coast, Basse Navarre inland, and Soule on the Pyrenees. It borders Gipuzkoa and Navarre on the south and Les Landes on the north.

Despite its small size (2,870 km^2) and population (262.311 inhabitants in 1999), the study of the economic structure of the Northern Basque Country is a difficult and necessarily incomplete task. This is mainly due to the absence of its own institutions, which would provide a framework for independent analysis. As a result, even statistics specific to this territory are lacking. The administrative division of the French state into macroregions makes it impossible to understand the data concerning the reality of the Basque Country: the Northern Basque Country is included in the region of Aquitaine, accounting for only 9% of the latter's population and 7% of its area. Moreover, the Northern Basque Country combines with Béarn to comprise the southern part of the Department of the Atlantic Pyrenees. The Northern Basque Country accounts for 43% of this department's population. The available data about the department does not provide much insight into the economic reality of the Northern Basque Country, since part of it groups Labourd and Nafarroa Behera on one hand, and Soule and Béarn on the other.

These deficiencies limit the scope of this study, since information related to the GDP and sectorial GAV are not released. In any case, some insight into the important features of the economic structure can be gained by looking at data about the labor market.

Currently, only unemployment figures and a general economic overview are released by the Bayonne chamber of commerce. The French Institute of Economics and Statistics (INSEE), however, was expected to publish some data about the territory for the first time in late 2000.

The available data therefore reflects the structure of the population in relation to the labor market. Distribution by territory will also be taken into account, since the differences between the coast and inland are increasing each year. Next, the structure of the population's occupation will provide insight into its main activities, and the main characteristics of the Basque productive structure will then be described.

OCCUPATION OF THE POPULATION IN THE BASQUE COUNTRY, BY SECTOR

The great changes in the productive structure of the Northern Basque Country throughout the nineteenth and twentieth centuries have brought about the differences between its two areas: whereas the inland is associated with agriculture, livestock breeding, and some small industries, the coast is renowned for fishing, some port-related industries, and, especially, tourism.

IN ANALYZING THE labor market (see Table 27-1), therefore, what is most striking is the overwhelming percentage of the employed population working in the services sector (72.2%), due largely to the importance of tourism and related activities (such as hotels and restaurants). Industry ranked second, but employed only 14.8% of the working population. Activities connected with the primary sector (agriculture, livestock breeding, fishing, timber) were third; with 6.3% of all employees in 1990—above both the rate in the Southern Basque Country and the EU average—this sector is very

Table 27-1
Distribution of the employed population, by sector (1999)

Sector	Northern Basque Country	FCN	BAC
Agriculture, livestock fishing, forests	6.3	6.5	2.5
Industry	14.8	31.4	31.8
Building	6.6	9.1	7
Services	72.2	53	58.7

Sources: INSEE (RP99) for the Northern Basque Country; Fundación BBV.

Table 27-2
Unemployment level in the Basque Country (1999)

Unemployed	Northern Basque Country	FCN	BAC
Unemployed	14,855	18,300	149,400
≤ 25 years	3,981 (26.8%)	4.200 (15%)*	32.60%
Total	13%	8.1	15.50%
Women	16%	14.3	22.70%
Men	10%	4.2	10.70%

Sources: Assedic and INSEE (1999) for the Northern Basque Country, INE (1999 and *2000) for the FCN, EUSTAT (1999) for the BAC.

important. Lastly, at 6.6% (just behind the primary sector), building was also relevant.

A comparison of the data of the north and south reveals that the majority of employment throughout the Basque Country is in the service sector. The north, with two-thirds of its population working in this broad, varied sector, stands out, distantly followed by the BAC and the FCN.

INDUSTRY WAS more important in the south, with the percentage of jobs in this sector twice that of the north. Navarre has surpassed the BAC in this sector, especially according to the most recent data. The significance of the building sector is comparable throughout the territories, ranging between 6.6% and 9.1% of the working population.

Lastly, the primary sector is still more important in the north than in the south, closely followed by Navarre; with only 2.5% the BAC was last.

UNEMPLOYMENT IN THE BASQUE COUNTRY

At 13% of the active-age population in 1999, the unemployment rate in the Northern Basque Country is higher than that of Navarre. This rate is much higher in the BAC (see Table 27-2), where unemployment increased throughout the 1990s (reaching a maximum of 22% in 1996, before beginning to descend).

The high unemployment among women in all Basque territories is noteworthy, 6 points higher than that among men in the north and triple that in Navarre. Women's initial increased presence in the labor market appears to begin with their inclusion in the unemployment statistics, which sometimes takes a long time. Unemployment also affects young people acutely, exceeding 25% in most of the territories. The lowest

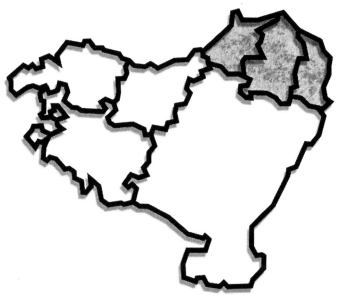

Detached trinity
The Northern Basque Country, also known as Ipar Euskal Herria, consists of three territories: Labourd, which is on the coast, Basse Navarre inland, and Soule on the Pyrenees. It borders Gipuzkoa and Navarre on the south, and Les Landes on the north.

---

appears to be in Navarre, followed by the Northern Basque Country.

ECONOMIC ACTIVITY AND GEOGRAPHIC DISTRIBUTION OF THE WORKING POPULATION
As the following data confirms, the imbalance between the coast and inland regions in the Northern Basque Country is increasing as a result of the concentration of the majority of the population on the coast. In 1999,

42.8% of the population lived in the Bayonne-Angelu-Biarritz (BAB) conurbation and 23.7% along the rest of Labourd's coast. Two-thirds of the population was therefore concentrated on the coast. Of the remaining, inland population, 18.9% lived in Labourd; 9.4% in Nafarroa Behera; and 5.1% in Soule. In other words, the farther inland, the fewer inhabitants. This tendency has become even more pronounced in the past decades, due to the greater opportunities for finding employment or studying on the coast. Many people have also ultimately left the Basque Country altogether.

AS NOTED, THE BAB conurbation accounts for nearly half of the Northern Basque Country's residents. It experienced a 20% population increase in the 1970s and 1980s, though in the 1990s it has diminished in importance as people have moved towards the rest of the Labourd coast. This is due to positive net migration, which has counteracted a widening deficit in its natural balance. Out of the existing complexity related to the study of migration, it is noteworthy that 52% of the immigrants come from outside of the Aquitaine region. Due to expensive housing, lack of universities, low demand for workers, and other factors, the tendency among young people raising families is to leave the district in favor of the periphery. Of the three BAB municipalities, Angelu has experienced the greatest population increase in recent decades. The increasing population of the surrounding municipalities is due to their proximity, and the difference in land and real estate prices also merits mention.

This district is the administrative center of the Northern Basque Country and an important focus of attraction for various economic activities, such as industrial, commercial, and service. Companies, especially those with more than 100 employees, tend to establish themselves in this area (85% of the Northern Basque Country's companies are located in the BAB).

Lastly, there is another economic space in which the different administrations are engaged in joint projects. Called the Bayonne–San Sebastian Conurbation, it extends from the BAB down to San Sebastian. The area is home to 620,000 people on the stretch of coast between these two cities. It has traditionally been a border contact area, with economic relationships and activity dependent upon close historical and cultural bonds, and differences in price of land, real estate, and consumer goods. This area has great potential to create neighboring ties for reasons of shared culture and the slow, but apparent, process of the dissolution of the state border separating them.

UNTIL A FEW years ago, people from the south, especially those living near the border, found going shopping or even buying a house in the Northern Basque Country attractive, because of the quality and variety of products, difference in interest rates, lower population density, and higher standard of living. According to 1994 data, 94% of those crossing the border cited shopping in the North as the or a chief motive. The majority, from Gipuzkoa (89.6%), lived close to the border and went to the seaside towns.

There was less movement in the other direction, since the only attractions in the Southern Basque Country were a few goods, such as alcohol, cigarettes, gasoline, and cars. Nevertheless, consumer behavior is changing. Malls similar to those in the north, often the main destination, are now being built in the south.

In summary, the lack of independent institutions prevents a more up-to-date, complete report on the Northern Basque Country's economic situation. It has been possible, however, to highlight specific features of its economic structure. Hopefully, in the years to come, the promise of more complete, periodic analyses of the Northern Basque Country's economy will become a reality.

Lesson twenty-seven

BIBLIOGRAPHY

Chambre de Commerce et d'Industrie de Bayonne Pay Basque. http://www.bayonne.cci.fr. m.

French Statistics Institute. http://www.insee.fr

Mailharrancin, E., and B. Soulé. 1996. *L'activité économique du Pays Basque Nord*. Ipareko.

LEARNING GOALS

1. Show the difficulty of getting accurate information about the economic situation of the Northern Basque Country.
2. Describe the main lines of employment of the active population of the Northern Basque Country and the characteristics of the unemployed.
3. Provide a panorama of the geographic distribution of the active population and recent tendencies.

WRITTEN LESSON FOR SUBMISSION

1. Taking previous chapters as a point of reference, compare the distribution of the active population, by sectors, in the Northern and Southern Basque Country, and locate them geographically.
2. When you look at the main tendencies of the geographic distribution of the active population in the Northern Basque Country, what trends, in your opinion, will mark the coming decade?

28 · The Northern Basque Country, part II

A FEATURE COMMON throughout Basque territory is the importance of small and midsize companies. Taking the companies in the nonfarming commercial sector in the Northern Basque Country as a basis, the 1990 data reveals that 68.8% of workers are employed in companies of under 50 workers, and only 3.96% are employed in companies of over 500; 12.8% of all employees work in companies with over 200 workers. This importance is due to the characteristics of the tertiary sector, the main source of work, in which most businesses are small.

Companies of more than 200 employed 21.5% of the workers in the Northern Basque Country's secondary sector in 1993. This means that, due to a few large aeronautics, mechanics, and electronics businesses, companies of this size are more important in this sector than in the commercial sector. These large companies reduced jobs throughout the 1980s, and they currently depend largely on foreign capital.

Another feature of the Basque business structure is therefore the importance of companies with foreign capital and belonging to large transnational industrial groups. It is estimated that over a third of the working population in the Northern Basque Country is employed in these large companies, which exist in all sectors (especially the most important ones) and provide subletting opportunities to small local businesses.

Table 28-1 shows the main activities of the service sector, by percentage of employees.

Within service (as noted, the leading sector), education, health, and social services (especially those devoted to the elderly) are the most prevalent, employ-

Table 28-1
Service sector employees, Northern Basque Country (%, 1999)

Activities	Northern Basque Country
Trade	15.3
Transportation	3.9
Insurance, finance, and real estate services	4.0
Enterprise services	8.6
Services to particular people	11.1
Education, health, and social services	20.3
Public administration services	9.1
Tertiary sector (total)	72.2

Source: INSEE (1999).

Table 28-2
Industrial employees, Northern Basque Country (%, 1999)

Activities	Northern Basque Country
Foodstuffs industry	2.9
Energy production and distribution	0.8
Intermediate goods industry	3.9
Capital goods industries	3.6
Consumer goods industries	3
Industrial sector (total)	14.3

Source: INSEE (1999).

ing 20.3% of the total working population, followed by trade services (15.3%). Those mainly directed to private individuals are also very important in the Northern Basque Country (11.1%). This is mainly due to the type of tourism promoted—designed for old people who can find peace and quiet in a beautiful, well-preserved, clean environment (with little industry), with a warm climate that makes it very suitable for health care and decreasing tension. Health centers therefore abound, especially near the sea.

Next come public administration services, including all collective services financed through taxes and social contributory payments, and therefore offered free or nearly free. Among them, the following merit mention: police, justice, and collective sports and cultural facilities (either public or administered by nonprofit private associations). Those services supplied to businesses have grown in importance in the last years (8.6% in 1999).

THE RELATIVE insignificance of both financial and real estate services is due to the economic structure of the Northern Basque Country.

Table 28-2 shows the main activities of the industrial sector, by percentage of employees. As can be seen, INSEE classifies industrial activities according to the type of goods produced. Industry in the Northern Basque Country is relatively unimportant, partly due to the development of tourism on the coast and the significance of farming inland. However, capital goods industries stand out in the sector, including large international electric and electronic component companies, such as Sony, SAT, Surgitec, and Télérad. The aeronautics industry is also important, including Dassault Aviation, which is significant but has been downsizing throughout the past decade.

Lean times
The conflicts among fishing boat owners from the Northern and Southern Basque Country have been caused by their different techniques; it has been a conflict not over territory, but over different models of exploiting fishing resources.
Engraving from Harold Hart: Trades and Professions.

The consumer goods industry is secondary, although footwear and furniture are still relevant. Despite the fact that jobs and even businesses have disappeared in the former, it is currently experiencing a resurgence inland. Next comes the intermediate goods industry, in which metal transformation is noteworthy, including companies such as SAFAM, ADA, Jean Neuhaus, and basic chemical activities.

FARMING AND LIVESTOCK IN THE NORTHERN BASQUE COUNTRY

Throughout Basque territory as a whole, there has been a decrease in the number of people involved in farming. Many have moved to urban areas to pursue other jobs and a different lifestyle. This has caused the depopulation of some rural areas as well as a concentration of production in towns and, in the case of the Northern Basque Country, on the coast. The Common Agriculture Policy developed by the EU has influenced this population shift by encouraging increased production as if agriculture were like any other industrial activity. Farming has therefore become intensively mechanized and the number of hands needed for production has declined. The result has been a quiet but constant reorganization of the sector.

DUE TO ITS longstanding inclusion within the EEC (and later EU), the north has suffered the consequences of common policies before. Although 6.3% remain involved in agriculture, the importance of the primary sector has diminished considerably in recent decades: 38.5% fewer people worked in this sector (including fishing) in 1990 than in 1975 and that trend has followed the same path during the 1990s. Services experienced a nearly identical increase during the same period. During the 1990s 15.8% of all farms disappeared, and the size of those in operation grew from an average of 12.5 hectares in 1975 to 23 hectares in 2000.

With respect to the chances of farm continuation, 41% of the people active in the sector have an heir; 17.6% of those with registered farms are under 35; and 14.7% of farmers between 35 and 59 are unmarried. Another widespread feature in both the north and south is that many farmers have a second job—in the Northern Basque Country, one out of five.

Lastly, as livestock breeding is the leading occupation, fodder and pasture represent the main activities of the sector; the land used for fodder production occupies 85% of all farmland.

THE FISHING SECTOR

Fishing is also suffering the consequences of the enforcement of an industrialized and profit-based model of catch in the Northern Basque Country. With the arrival of new techniques, such as pelagic and trawl line nets, traditional fishing is disappearing. It is being replaced by a more industrial fishing sector that seeks to recoup the huge investment required by the new techniques. The monetary value of the catch in the two main ports in the Northern Basque Country, Saint-Jean-de-Luz and Hendaye, has been declining in recent years. Moreover, the port of Bayonne is relatively unimportant to fishing. In order to compensate for its dearth of activity, some people have taken up algae picking; a good source of supplementary income.

ON THE OTHER hand, despite a rivalry with ports in the Northern Basque Country, those in Gipuzkoa (mainly Pasaia's) are used for unloading 20% of the catch of Saint-Jean-de-Luz and 40% of Hendaye's, according to 1996 data.

The conflicts among fishing boat owners from the Northern and Southern Basque Country have been caused by their different techniques; it has been a conflict not over territory, but over different models of exploiting fishing resources. Some boat owners from the north agree with the traditional methods, while the current degree of competition leads some from the south to disregard the natural limitation of sealife resources and to favor the pelagic and trawl line techniques.

Lesson twenty-eight

BIBLIOGRAPHY
Club de Prospective. 1994. *Pays Basque 2010*.
French Statistics Institute. http://www.insee.fr.
Mailharrancin, E., and B. Soulé. 1996. *L'activité économique du Pays Basque Nord*. Ipareko.

LEARNING GOAL
Outline the salient features of the economic framework in the Northern Basque Country, stressing the major activities developed in each sector.

WRITTEN LESSON FOR SUBMISSION
Compare and contrast, sector by sector, the primary occupations of the active population in the Northern Basque Country with those in its southern homologue. Keep the previous chapters in mind.

List of abbreviations

BAC: Basque Autonomous Community
BBK: Bilbao Bizkaia Kutxa (Basque Saving Bank)
BBVA: Banco Bilbao Vizcaya Argentaria
BSCH: Banco Santander Central Hispano
CAN: Caja de Ahorros de Navarra (Navarre Saving Bank)
FCN: Foral Community of Navarre
LSC: Labor Stock Companies
MPTs: Millions of pesetas
PTS: Pesetas (Spanish currency until 2002)
SMEs: Small and Midsize Companies

In this book "billion" follows the American convention of meaning a thousand millions.

Endnotes

1. At present, the Northern Basque Country is juridically in France and the Southern Basque Country in Spain. As the reader will note, the inexactitude of the cultural and political boundaries makes description problematic. Throughout this book, a compromise is made in naming conventions: French is used to refer to places juridically in France; Spanish to refer to those in Navarre; and Euskera, or Basque, to refer to those in Araba, Bizkaia and Gipuzkoa; in this latter group, exceptions are made for Bilbao and San Sebastian, due to their currency in English, and the Basque capital of Vitoria-Gasteiz, commonly hyphenated to include its name in both languages. See chapter 6, note 2.
2. As the reader will see, the BAC is composed of the provinces of Araba, Bizkaia, and Gipuzkoa, the result of a 1979 Statute of Autonomy. The FCN is the result of a subsequent, single-territory statute covering Navarre.
3. Although these programs include a specific list of areas and lines of technology, they do have a certain flexibility. This leaves room to accommodate previously unidentified needs that may emerge during the plan's development.
4. Technological centers in Navarre: CETENASA (Technological Centers of Navarre: laser, metrology, production and electronic, materials, automation and computers) and AIN (Association of Industry in Navarre). Sectorial Centers in Navarre: EVENA (Viticulture and enology), CTNCV (National Technical Center of Preserved Vegetables), Agrarian Laboratory of the Government in Navarre, Lacteal Institute, LENSA (Construction Sector).

5. ICT has recognized the functions of an Office of Research Output Transfer (an industrial liaison office) by the General Secretary of the National Plan.
6. The preparation and development of this plan was supported by the European Commission through the RIS (Regional Innovation Strategies) Program of the XVI General Directorship of Regional Policy.
7. MCC was able to solve finance problems, common to all cooperatives, through the creation of a cooperative bank: Caja Laboral Popular.
8. The Professional School (Escuela Profesional)—an independent, democratically managed school open to the youth of the region—was founded by Arizmendiarrieta in 1943. Residents, regional small and midsize companies, and local authorities supported the school's creation. It is currently called the Mondragon Eskola Politeknikoa (Mondragón Politechnical School).
9. The cooperatives Talleres Arrasate (1958), Copreci (1962), and Ederlan (1963) were closely related to Ulgor both at the outset and later. Ulgor is currently Fagor Electrodomésticos, and Talleres Arrasate is Fagor Arrasate.
10. Arizmendiarrieta's idea of creating a new credit cooperative was initially not supported by his collaborators.
11. Initially, Ikerlan's research was funded by Mondragón cooperatives. Since 1982, however, the Basque government has joined many other R&D organizations to finance it.
12. In 1985, the name Ularco was changed to Fagor, a name used henceforth by all companies of the former Ularco commercial group: Fagor Electrodomésticos (formerly, Ulgor S. Coop.), Fagor Electrónica S. Coop. (formerly, Electrotécnica), Fagor Arrasate (for-

merly, Arrasate S. Coop.), and Fagor Ederlan S. Coop. (formerly, Ederlan).
13. An economy's export propensity is measured by the exports compared to the GDP.
14. Special mention must be made of the contribution of Mailharrancin and Soulé (1996); more generally, we would like to acknowledge the IPAR-EKO conference organized by the HEMEN association in Bayonne in 1996–97 for its great interest in our study.

Pictures

School of Thomas Bewick. From Thomas Hugo: *Bewick's Woodcuts*. L. Reeve & Co., London, 1870. 125
Jens Bonnke, Artville, Madison, 1998. 68, 79, 207
Seymour Chwast, Flat File Editions Inc., New York, 1995. 151, 175, 202
Gustave Doré: *The Doré Bible Illustrations*. Dover, New York, 1974. 120
Ingo Fast, Artville, Madison, 1997. 51, 192
Harold Hart: *The Illustrator's Handbook*, Hart Publishing, New York, 1977. 8, 113, 197
———: *Trades and Professions*, Galahad Books, New York, 1977. 249
Jim Harter: *Animals, Pictorial Archive*. Dover, New York, 1979. 120, 130
———: *Men, A Pictorial Archive* from Nineteenth-Century Sources. Dover, New York, 1980. 84, 166
Johann George Heck: *Pictorial Archive of Nature & Science*, Dover, New York, 1982. 21, 139
———: *The Complete Encyclopedia of Illustration* (1851 facsimile), Park Lane, New York, 1979. 28, 44
———: *Heck's Pictorial Archive of Military Science, Geography, and History*, Dover, New York, 1994. 21
Illustrator's Reference Manual. Chartwell Books, Seacaucus, New Jersey. 161
Robin Jareaux, Artville, Madison, 1997. 74, 100, 224
G. Brian Karas, Artville, Madison, 1998. 146
Nüremberg Chronicle, 1493. 233
PhotoDisc, Inc., Seattle, 1995. 100, 157
Punch, London, no date. 13
Jennifer Thermes, Artville, Madison, 1998. 108, 214
Iñaki Uriarte, 221.

Index

A

Aceros de Llodio, 26
Acerías y Forjas de Azkoitia, 26
admissible total catch (ATC) brought about great reduction in Basque fishing, 129
adoption of technology by Basque industries via network of technology and support R&D within companies, 145
aeronautics, mechanics and electronics businesses: employed 21.5% of workers in Northern Basque Country's secondary sector in 1993, 246
AESA, in 1969 La Naval (Sestao) and Euskalduna merged with Cadiz Astilleros to create, 52
Agency for Industrial Promotion and Restructuring (SPRI) promotion and restructuring of Basque industry, 144
agricultural sector
    Bizkaia, Gipuzkoa, and Araba added value (constant pesetas) decreased from 12.3% of the total (1955) to 8.8% (1964) to 5.1% (1975), 35
    production decrease to lowest level, 38%, in 1995, 118
agriculture, plays a larger role in southern Araba and the FCN, 121
airports: Bilbao (Sondika), Vitoria-Gasteiz (Foronda), San Sebastian (Hondarribia), Pamplona (Noain), and Biarritz, 114. See also Basque airports.
Altos Hornos de Vizcaya
    founded in 1902, 21
    importance in postwar years of, 27–28
Altsasu, 231
anchovy
    principal spring catch of coastal fishing, 132
    reduction in the quota on, 129
ancien régime main economic resources: agriculture, pasture rents and livestock supplemented by iron forging, fishing and commercial traffic, 10

Index

Angelu experienced the greatest population increase in recent decades, 243
Anglet, 236
Araba, 7
    Concierto Económico, 16
    confiscate church land, 14
    deputation five year industrial plan of 1971 to 1975, 39
    economic growth selection as BAC's administrative capital and availability of large sites for development of economic activity, 235
    industrialization in, 22, 27
Araba, Bizkaia, and Labourd sharpest demographic imbalance with most on coast, 231
Aristrain, 26
Astilleros Españoles S.A., foundation in 1969 of, 38
Atarrabia, 236
autonomous police force jurisdiction exclusive to the Basque Country, 69

B

Babcock Wilcox, 26
BAC, 253
Banco de Bilbao, 30
    founded in 1856, 21
Banco de Comercio, founded in 1891, 21
Banco de San Sebastian, founded in 1862, 21
Banco de Tolosa, 24
Banco de Vitoria, 24
Banco de Vizcaya, 30
    founded in 1901, 24
Banco Guipuzcoano, 24
banking flourished not only to economic development but also to Spain's neutrality, 24
    reducing investment in industry thus exposing to very high interest rates, indebtedness, and general financial worries, 52
banks, factors that contributed to the success of Bizkaia, 21–22

Basque
    agriculture diminished while industry increased in 60s and 70s, 42
    airports: Bilbao (Sondika), Vitoria-Gasteiz (Foronda), San Sebastian (Hondarribia), Pamplona (Noain), and Biarritz, 114. See also airports
    political divisions, 254
    urbanization process belated in comparison to that elsewhere in Europe, 229
Basque Autonomous Community (BAC)
    areas of employment and social security are most relevant, but also most difficult to transfer, 84
    industry currently exports 29% of the autonomous community's GDP to foreign countries, 214
    loss of industrial jobs, from 1975 to 1985, 49
    manufacturing rate rather low in relative specialization, 141
    specialized in intermediate goods, 139
    R&D technology centers main component, 164–165
    relatively specialized in steel, metal goods, machinery, rubber and plastics, 140
    transportation problems: decrease in mobility of goods, excessive spatial concentration, existing framework, great investment in short period of time, suffers from degree of democratic deficit, 115–116
Basque banking, through influence on industry, played a dynamic mid century role, 32
Basque coast became overcrowded with tourists by the beginning of the twentieth century, 12
Basque companies, shortages in 1940s effected, 26
Basque Cooperative Movement, 39–40
Basque Country, dominant features of, 7–8
Basque economy
    boost in the expansion of new mass consumer goods, 34
    fifty percent of the GDP comes from Bizkaia, 214
    increasingly externally oriented, 76
    integration is taking place mainly within the European Union, 78

joint ventures as form of public participation during the 1960s and 1970s, 38
rather open to foreign trade, 78
Basque farm
  permanent name and 4 to 8 hectares of property, 7
  significant decrease in income affected the classes, 13
Basque fleet's spring coastal fishing 52% reduction in the quota on anchovy had an impact on, 129
Basque industries
  less financially adaptable than their European competitors, 137
Basque institutions: joint responsibility, tax harmonization, Insertion in international treaties, Effective pressure, free circulation of capital, 66–67
Basque manufacturers exhibit a lack of managerial and business culture, 49
Basque oligarchy in the state economic and political network, role of, 40
Basque production had to maintain close foreign ties to provide markets for surplus goods and access to those in short supply, 43
Basque taxes: joint responsibility, coordination, insertion, effect pressure, respect, 66–67
Basque Technology Network incorporate all the agents (including university) into the R&D infrastructure and coordinate their participation, 149
Basque urban hierarchy: 1. Greater Bilbao, 2. San Sebastian, Vitoria-Gasteiz, Pamplona, and Bayonne, 3. Eibar, Irun, Bermeo, Durango, Altsasu, Tudela, et al., 231
"Basque Y" as three BAC capital cities with high-speed links to the rest of Spain and Portugal and to the European high-speed network, 112
Basse Navarre, 7, 10, 238, 242
Basse Navarre and Soule: most towns have under 500 occupants and these numbers are on the decline, 231
Bayonne, 10, 12, 231, 239
  depended on the development of the district under its dominion, 229

export of iron, coal and steel from, 19
great coast / inland divide with demographic dynamism and economic activity, 236
Labourd and Basse Navarre oriented towards, 232
since 1998 is France's ninth most active seaport, 114
trade through port of, 19
Bayonne-San Sebastian Conurbation: potential to create neighboring ties for reasons of shared culture, 244
BBK, 253
BBVA, 253
Bermeo (Bizkaia), 231
port of most modern and profitable part of the Basque fleet, 133
Bessemer method: new Mining Laws of 1859 enabled the exploitation of mines via the, 19
Bewick, School of Thomas, engraving, 125
Biarritz, 12, 13, 236
at end of nineteenth century, tourism growth evidence, 18
population growth in, 18
Bilbao, 231
and San Sebastian: center of commercialization, 10–11
dominant position relative to other ports (Bermeo, Lekeitio, and Castro), 107
northern Iberian peninsula's largest and most important metropolitan area, 232
one of two leading ports of Southern Basque Country, 112
promotion of tertiary sector and technological renewal of industry, 234
redistribution of goods throughout Europe, 10
register of cargo ships at, 20
Stock Exchange: development of variable income market for small and midsize companies, 209
billion, a thousand millions, 253
Bizkaia, 7
Concierto Económico, 16
confiscate church land, 14
export of iron ore from, 19
industrialization in, 22, 23, 27

most dynamic part, in 1960, of the Southern Basque Country, 31
population increase in, 22
Bizkaia and Gipuzkoa, 9
exportation of manufactured goods from, 32
population increase, between 1900 and 1940 largest, 24
Bizkaia industry problems in 1940s due to shortage of supplies caused by autarkic home policies and effects of European war, 26
Bonnke, Jens, illustrations by, 68, 79, 207
Boucou, furnaces installed in, 18
bourgeois liberal regime: legal equality, elimination of tax and feudal privileges, constitutional-liberal political system, and economic unity of monarchy, 13
bourgeois liberal society: disappearance of feudalism and adoption of model inspired by liberal principles, 12
BSCH, 253
Burlata, 236
business activities in which academics are engaged: Large-scale scientific projects (56.2%), Research contracts (47.6%), extrauniversity teaching (40.9%), 169

C

Caja Laboral
creation of a popular bank, 255
financial services, technical (Enterprise Division) and social services, 183
Cámara de Comptos of Navarre, controls public accounts but with an even longer tradition than BAC's Hacienda Foral, 70
CAN, 253
capital movement and the development of wider-range markets, need to determine space in European Union for, 85
cargo ships for Vizcaya ore, cause the construction of new, 20
Carlist Wars, 14–16
catering is a rapidly growing industry increasing in relative importance due to recent growth in tourism, 97
chemicals
sector with highest foreign participation, 36

status in 1950, for Bizkaia and Gipuzkoa, of, 29
church property in southern Basque territory: confiscation in early nineteenth century of, 14
Chwast, Seymour, illustrations by, 151, 175, 202
cities included in international networks will have great advantages over those cities and territories excluded, 225–226
combination of unemployment and early retirement facilitated removal of hundreds of thousands of employees from job, 198
Common Agrarian Policy (CAP), 124
common business activities of academics: large-scale scientific projects (56.2%), research contracts (47.6%), extrauniversity teaching (40.9%), 169
Common Fishing Policy (CFP)ensuring fishing livelihoods and reasonable prices, 129
companies active in the credit sector: credit companies, savings banks, credit cooperatives, 203–205
Concierto Económico,
    Bizkaia and Gipuzkoa recovered, in 1981, with the state, 53
    territory would contribute to state treasury in accordance to its wealth, 16
conflicts among fishing boat owners caused by northerners agreeing on traditional methods while southerners disregard natural limitation, 251
construction of steel mills caused by: convergence of capital in space and time, iron ore, adequate technology, iron markets, 20–21
consumer goods, prices went up due to shortage of, 30–31
cooperatives, decision making and a share in benefits is not linked to the capital contribution of each member, 175
credit
    companies: banks, savings banks, credit cooperatives, 203
    cooperatives require their members financial needs met first, 205
crisis and reorganization as main features of the Basque fishing sector, 131

D

Dassault Aviation in North Basque, important but downsizing for past decade, 248

decisions made through assemblies around parishes or representatives elected in towns, villages, parishes or brotherhoods, 10

Decree of Espartero (1841): moved the borders to Irun, abolished foral free trade, and brought the Juntas Generales to their end, 16

deep-sea fishing
  hake the most prized, 133
  most modern and profitable part of the Basque fleet, 133

Deputations and the Basque Government, Distribution of the Share Between, 67–68

development model, must take into account spatial and social consequences of, 226

Distribution Group of MCC, 186–187

Doré, Gustave, cliffs from, 120

double duty, Credit cooperatives have a dual status both cooperative associations and credit companies, 207

Durango, 231

E

economy's per capita income levels, crisis of 1975–85 impacted strongly on, 60

Eibar, 231

Errenteria, 234

Esteban Orbegozo, 26

European Union evolution: determine space for both capital movement and development of wider-range markets, differences that prevent more unified government, reluctance on the part of richer countries to share wealth, 85–86

Euskalduna shipbuilding, 23, 28, 29

Euskoiker university-business foundation manage contracts signed by academics and businesses or other organizations, 168

EuskoTren provides local service for three Basque capitals, 111–112

F

Fagor, Ularco was changed to, 255
Fagor Arrasate was Talleres Arrasate, 255
farm sector stability dependent upon continuation of family, self sufficiency in food production, 7
Fast, Ingo, watercolors by, 51, 192
FCN, 253
FEVE, railroads that cover most of northern Spain, 111
Financial Group of MCC, 185–186
financial sector, channel savings of economic units with a surplus towards deficit and in need of funding, 201
Firestone, 26
fishing
    boat construction, growth in the 1950's of, 251
    conflict between different models of exploiting resource, 251–252
    production focuses in Bizkaia and Giipuzkoa on, 121
Fishing Strategic Plan (PEP), renewal, modernization, structural adjustment of fleet and fishing techniques, 133
footwear in Hasparren, emergence of, 18
Foral Deputations
    have a series of agreements with government of state, 65
    most common allocations are those dealing with road infrastructure and social programs, 67
foral system
    determined relationship between private property and collective use of land, 9
    law abolishing in 1876, 16
four kinds of projects: proposed by technology centers, proposed by groups within clusters, between supply and demand, proposed by companies, 148
freedom of movement in international markets, capital and financial resources are currently the best indicator of, 73
French Revolution of 1789 in Basque country, caused elimination of both birthright laws and the collective use of common lands, 11
furnaces installed in Boucou, emergence of, 18

G

Gandarias, a member of the mining bourgeoise who became shipowners, 20
General Law of the Mines, 15
geographic inequality and high concentration of agricultural subsidies estimated that 4% of the farmers currently receive 40% of the subsidies, 124
Gipuzkoa, 7,
    Concierto Económico, 16
    confiscate church land, 14
    industrialization in, 22
    population increase within, 22
Gipuzkoa and Navarre: greater distribution of population and more balanced urban systems, 231
Gipuzkoa Industrialization greater decentralization and sectorial diversity than in Bizkaia, 22
globalization
    encapsulates the degree of internationalization of current economy, 72
    multiplicity of international factors that coalesced during the 1990s, 72
great investment within a very short period of time construction of large infrastructural networks requires, 115
growing concern for higher quality goods for a demanding market, 123

H

Hart, Harold, engravings by, 8, 113, 197, 249
Harter, Jim, engravings by, 84, 120, 130, 166
Hasparren, emergence of footwear industry in, 18
Heck, Johann George, engravings by, 21, 28, 44, 139
Hecle, engraving from, 44
Hego-Uribe, included in area of greater Bilbao, 234
Hernani, 234
high unemployment among women in all Basque territories 6 points higher than that among men in the north and triple that in Navarre, 241

Huarte, Navarrese capitalist, 32
Huici, Navarrese capitalist, 32

I

Illustrator's Reference Manual, photograph from, 160

increased population density of coast, accompanied by major trend towards depopulation of inland areas of Northern Basque Country, 12

Industrial Group of MCC, 186

industrial model of the Northern Basque Country weak due to dependence on agriculture based on small landed property and capital, trade, and services, 19

industrial productive specialization in the Southern Basque Country influenced by the process of accumulation on a state level, 42

Industrial Technology Plan 1993–96, concentrated regressive sectors, 138

industry in the BAC highly specialized in regressive sectors, 142

infrastructural and transportation policy existing institutional and jurisdictional framework conditioned, 116

infrastructural networks necessary but insufficient condition for economic growth of region, 99

instruments of the science and technology plan: infrastructure, R&D Projects, Technology Innovation, training, 150

integrated market demands require: need to respect deficit limits, need to promote less developed regions of market, 103

internal economic development: business class training, ethics of work, employers & unions cooperation, educational system & workforce qualification, 97

internationalization of large infrastructural networks promotes already consolidated centers, 100

IPAR-EKO conference, 256

iron ore extraction, slowed due to high prices and low demand, 27

Irun, 231

J

Jareaux, Robin, watercolors by, 74, 100, 224
joined to support the new liberal regime: segment of aristocracy, bourgeoisie, civil servants and liberal professionals, minority among high clergy, 16
joint ventures, most relevant form of public participation in Basque economy during 1960s and 1970s, 38

K

Karas, G. Brían, drawing by, 146

L

Labor Market, number of working individuals has shattered all records, 217
Labor Stock Companies (LSCs): small businesses in computer science, engineering, business services, technical assistance, and transportation, 179–180
Labourd, 7, 10, 238, 242, 243
   focused on species to be canned, 128
Lasarte-Oria, 234
Law for the Renewal of the Fishing Fleet, increase in capacity under, 128
Ley Paccionada (Pacted Law) of 1841, dismantled the foral system in Navarre, 16
limits to sovereignty: oligopolistic concentrations, central monetary policies, reluctance to share wealth, cultural-linguistic-historical differences, 86
livestock and forests, the north of the FCN, and Araba production, 121
LSC, 253

M

machine-tool industry growth in 1940s and 1950s, 29
manufactured goods, significant export in the 1950s of, 32
market, structure of an integrated demands coordination and the creation of directives over infrastructural links, 103
Mauleon, emergence of sandal making in, 18

Mauleon and Hasparren, shoemaking became industrialized in, 11
metal manufacturing, continued to grow at the expense of consumer goods, 42
metropolis centers: ample consumer market, activity related to management, job market diversified, 220
metropolis's international character: telecommunication networks, mobility of population, communication nodes within large infrastructural networks, 222–223
metropolitan area administrative levels have different jurisdictions, 227
Metropolitan Revival as the axis of development policies, 223–225
minimum insertion income (IMI), 196
mining business energized railway and ship companies for shipping ore, 20
mining laws of 1825 and 1859, 19
Miranda de Ebro and Logroño, influence of territorial capitals although southern Araba and Ribera in Navarre fall under the influence of, 232
mobility of goods results in a decrease of services and citizens, 115
Mondragon Cooperative Corporation (MCC). See Mondragon Cooperative Group
Mondragon Cooperative Group: financing (into which Caja Laboral and Lagun-Aro were integrated) and business (industrial, services and food, and agricultural), 185
Mondragon Eskola Politeknikoa, 255
MPTs, 253

N

Nafarroa Behera; 243
Navarre, 7, 9
   confiscate church land, 14
   industrial promotion in 1964–74, 39
   industrialization in, 22, 27

Navarre's industrialization process
  continuing significance of force from agricultural sector, 110–111, 154
  international & intraregional routes, 110–111
network of roads
  international, connection with main centers, interregional, local, 110–111
new cargo ships, need to transport iron ore required, 20
Northern Basque Country, 7
  agriculture declining while intensively mechanized, 250
  capital goods industries in, 248
  coast renowned for fishing, port-related industries, and tourism, 239
  dynamism & economic activity on coast while inland population declining, 236
  fishing, with arrival of new techniques traditional fishing disappearing, 251
  footwear and furniture experiencing a resurgence inland, 249
  interior has agriculture, livestock breeding and small industries, 239
  Labourd and Basse Navarre are oriented toward Bayonne, 232
  service sector, overwhelming percentage working in (72.2%), 239
  Soule is oriented towards Pau, 232
  socioeconomic framework of: iron forging, fishing, trade in Bayonne, industries and artisanship, 10
  tourism and related activities, importance of, 239
  towns under influence of Bayonne and Pau (Bearn), 232
Nuestra Señora del Carmen (1855), new steel mill considered pioneers of modern steel industry, 20
Nuestra Señora de la Merced (1846), new steel mill considered pioneers of modern steel industry, 20
Nüremberg Chronicle, 1493, woodcut from, 233

O

Office of Research Output Transfer (OTRI), 255
  manage contracts of university academics and businesses or others, 168
overfishing, technological innovations related to ships and fishing tackle (trawl line) were responsible by end of 19th century for, 128

P

Pamplona, 231
  center of balanced urban network, 235
  industrialization in the 1950s, 31
  promoted city's centralizing pull, 236
Pamplona and Vitoria-Gasteiz, industrialization in the 1950s of, 31
Paris-Bordeaux railway extended to Bayonne and Irun, 12
Pasaia, 234
  one of two leading ports of Southern Basque Country, 112
Pau, Soule is oriented towards, 232
PhotoDisc, Inc., photographs from, 100, 157
popular initiatives: business organizations and institutions are given preference over, 227
Population crisis due to migration and poverty cause decrease until first Carlist war, 15
possibility of producing higher quality goods for a demanding market, 123
Potasas de Navarra, 38
private sector participation in financing projects, 101
private social welfare coverage technology model with high level of public funding, 147,
privileged cities, international functions are concentrated within, 226
profit margin of the productive sector in Bizkaia, Gipuzkoa, and Araba rose at an annual average rate of 3.5%, 34
Programs: basic research, horizontal technology, specific technology, 152
promoter agent for research, University Clinic of the University of Navarre, 162

PTS, 253
public participation, mechanisms to promote are completely inefficient, 227
public subsidies (193–194): extending benefits, protecting people not covered by social security, social security benefits may not be sufficient, 193–194
Punch, engraving from, 13

Q

Quota, certain amount of money should be paid to the central government for funding activities out of their jurisdiction, 66

R

relative specialization, when gross added value is higher than normal rate, 138
RENFE, Basque Country is linked to all the most important Spanish cities by, 111
Research Regional Plan of Navarre (PRINA), promote a research culture within the region, 158

S

San Sebastian, 11, 231
    economic crisis had a negative impact and subsequent projects attempted to renew the city, 234
sandal-making in Mauleon, emergence of, 18
Science and Technology Plan 1997–2000
    instruments of, 150
    programs as basic research, horizontal technology and specific technology, 152
    requirements for, 149
scientific and technological institute (ICT) to facilitate contracts and provide service to companies, 161
Sefanitro, created to produce parts for the AHV furnaces, 26
service industry presence: underscores progress of services induced by the concentration of population and great impact of industrial decline, 91
shipbuilding, growth in the 1940s and 1950s of, 28–29

shortage of facilities gives rise to large differences in provision of social services, 45
Siderurgia del Mediteráneo, take over by AHV, 27
SMEs, 253
social and economic agents, infrastructural project suffers from a degree of democratic deficit in, 116
social economy as group of private companies whose common activities are: producing, benefit share and decision making, 172
social security, combination of unemployment benefits and early retirement facilitated relatively "painless" removal of hundreds of thousands of employees from job, 192
Social Spending in the Basque Country, 197–198
    increase in social security benefits as a consequence of growth of salaries increase in unemployment benefits longer life expectancy social welfare increase in benefits, unemployment, demographic changes caused by longer life expectancy, 198
    where system in primarily private, 190
    where system is universalist and covered by income taxes, 190–191
    where system depends upon contribution and covered by contributive payments, 191
Sociedad Española de Construccion Naval, 23
SODENA, created in 1984 the Agency for the Development of Navarre, 53
Somorrostro, mining zone of, 19
Sony, SAT, Surgitec, and Télérad, capital goods in North Basque Country, 248
Sota y Aznar, member of the mining bourgeoisie who became shipowners, 20
Soule, 7, 10, 238, 242, 243
Southern Basque Country
    Bizkaia, Gipuzkoa, Araba and Navarre, 7
    foral system determined relationship between private property and collective use of land, 9
    Franco's government seems to have been bent on discriminating against, 37

leader in normative development of minimum insertion income, 195
public investments role played by Foral Deputations, 39
recent supremacy of service industry within economy of, 93
until mid 1990s livestock always predominated over agriculture, 121
Spanish Constitution from a Socioeconomic Viewpoint:developed capitalist state, absolute jurisdiction over arenas controlled by state, Constitutional Jury, 65
Spanish social security system: contributory benefits, compensate people in poverty, public subsidies, partly private, 193–194. See also social welfare
Spanish state retained important regulatory functions, sovereignty over many jurisdictions, foreign trade relationships, and coordination in many areas, 63
spatial reorganization: financial institutions based in cities, new technologies provide expansion possibilities, traditional industries lost ground, 219
SPRI's initial years providing aid to companies experiencing great difficulties, 145
stagflation, combination of stagnation of production with inflation, 57
states can and do maintain their reason for being, 86
State monetary policy: very restrictive between 1977 and 1992, lack of public companies, and foreign investment, 52
steel mills, factors that contributed to construction of, 20–21
Stock Exchange of Bilbao, one of Spain's four stock markets, 208
structure of an integrated market requires respect for macroeconomic orientations and need to promote the development of less advanced regions, 103

T

Talleres Euskalduna, 26
Technical Institutes of Management (ITG) good agricultural assistance services are available through, 123
Technological Plan of Navarre
   facilitate access to new technologies, 158

sectorial and thematic projects, 159
technological policy, adapt R&D infrastructure to meet company demand and articulate demand through the clusters, 147
Technologic Strategy Unit, management unit designed to implement technology policy of Department of Industry, 147
technology centers, BAC's R&D sector main components, 164–165
Thermes, Jennifer, map by, 108, illustration by, 214
timber production, price rise encouraged increase in fellings, 122
town councils (Southern Basque country), sold off common lands to make payments, 15
trade became basic sector because of increased production and commercialization of steel productions, 10
Trans-European networks, as a connection among centers of some relevance, 100
transfer role, institutions that channel a surplus towards those with a deficit, 202
Tudela, 231
tuna
 against limits upon, 131
 fished from coastal fishing in the Summer, 132
Txoriherri, included in area of greater Bilbao, 234
typical problems of SMCs: insufficient capacity for innovation, commercialization / foreign-market penetration, training / management deficiencies, and financing, 178

U

Uharte, 236
Ulgor, now Fagor Electrodomesticos, 255
unemployment as most critical problem to be solved by economic growth, 102
University / Private obstacles: business funds, unaffiliated, answer company needs, with university technical departments, relationships not fluid, 169–170

University of Navarre's R&D services commercialized by CIFA (Center of Applied Chemistry Research), IBA (Applied Biology Institute), & CINDEB (Biomedical R&D Center), 161
University of the Basque Country most important higher-education institution in the Basque Country, 166
University Reform Law (URL), departments allowed to perform scientific, technical, or artistic jobs, 167
Unquinesa, founded to supply coal to AHV, 26
Uranga, Mikel Gomez, biography of, 2
Uriarte, Iñaki, photograph by, 221

V

Vidrieras de Llodio, 26
Vitoria-Gasteiz, 231
    airport, 114
    industrialization in the 1950s, 31
    selection as BAC's administrative capital and sites for economic activity, 235

W

welfare state helps increase national identity and unity, 83
woodcutter, in Araba and Navarra old-growth species are still important for, 125
work cooperatives problems: insufficient capacity for innovation, problems of commercialization and foreign-market penetration, training and management deficiencies, financing problems, 178
worker standard of living declining in the 1940s, 30
working class, general strike effected in 1962, 47

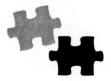

Colophon

This book was edited by John Hammett and indexed by Lawrence Feldman. Begoña Garcia-Saenz, Yolanda Jubeto, and Eva Velasco helped prepare and check the text. It was laid out and produced by Gunnlaugur SE Briem, who also designed the typeface, BriemAnvil.

It was printed and bound by Fidler Doubleday of Ann Arbor, Michigan.

The Basque Studies textbook series

1. Guggenheim Bilbao Museoa: Museums, Architecture, and City Renewal
2. Modern Basque History: Eighteenth Century to the Present
3. Basque Economy: From Industrialization to Globalization
4. Cyberculture in Euskal Herria
5. Basque Culture: Anthropological Perspectives
6. Basque Language, Society, and Culture
7. Basque Cinema: An Introduction
8. Basque Diaspora Studies